The Immigrants' New Camera:
A Family Collection

Other works by Maryfrances Wagner

Bandaged Watermelons and Other Rusty Ducks
Tonight Cicadas Sing
Salvatore's Daughter
Red Silk
Light Subtracts Itself
Dioramas
Pouf
The Silence of Red Glass

Co-Edited Anthologies

The Whirlybird Anthology of Greater Kansas City Poets
Missouri Poets: An Anthology

Of *Salvatore's Daughter:*

Maryfrances Wagner writes beautifully and lovingly from her Italian-American heritage, with its emphasis on family and neighborhood, on tradition and continuity, and on humanity's bond with the natural world. In a voice that is sometimes melancholy but never bitter or self-pitying, she moves from a theme of mutability and loss to one of renewal through family and romantic love. These poems consistently engage one with their insight and compassion, their fresh, straightforward language, and their concrete particularity. *Salute* to *Salvatore's Daughter!*

> William Trowbridge
> Editor of *The Laurel Review*
> Author of *O Paradise*

Of *Red Silk:*

I have admired the work of Maryfrances Wagner for more than twenty years, as have the legions of her students and readers. Now the publication of *Red Silk* is cause for our celebration, for here are the best of her new poems, arranged as both a personal memoir and a cultural history of America's past four decades. Each section of this powerful book becomes its own narrative episode.... In the end, Maryfrances Wagner knows the hardest knowledge: that the personal is the political, as the erotic is the elegiac.

> David Baker, Poetry Editor, *Kenyon Review*

Of *Light Subtracts Itself:*

With an extraordinary eye for imagery and hard-earned knowledge of the human condition, Wagner gives us in *Light Subtracts Itself* poems that smolder with loss and yet remind us of the joy of being. Your heart will sign on with these poems that explore subjects as diverse as death, early morning commutes, and the alchemy of light. Glimmering with the physical things of the world, offering *a stepladder to the possible,* Wagner's fifth collection takes us back to awe and wonder.

> Jo McDougall
> Author of *Dirt* and *Satisfied with Havoc*

Of *Dioramas*

Like the dioramas she invokes in the title poem, Maryfrances Wagner recreates views and perspectives for us to study and cherish. Included in her vignettes are the childhood traumas, the neighborhood legend-making, the treasured or rejected hand-me-downs of an Italian-American family. With skill and compassion she brings us into the classroom of dispossessed students. Her observant, musical poems are equally at home in the complicated theatre of human culture or outdoors with a *bacchanal* of cicadas on a summer night. The range of her view-finding is impressive as is her precision in using ordinary domestic objects to conjure disappearing eras and poignant memories.

> Donald Levering,
> Author of *The Water Leveling with Us*

Of *Pouf*:

Maryfrances Wagner's talent and years at the honing wheel dance through *Pouf.* These poems present an unforgettable character, Aunt Mary, who lives through the lively language of her best years of highballs, lobster, Uncle Johnny, and Frank Sinatra; all made more vivid through the lens of the nursing home to which age has assigned her. Although few poets could pull off this combination, Wagner not only does so, but delights the reader in the process, while staying true to Aunt Mary's wish, *I want people/to talk about how good I looked even dead.*

> Trish Reeves, *Returning the Question* –
> Cleveland State University Poetry Center Prize

Of *The Silence of Red Glass:*

Maryfrances Wagner writes poems that cherish, reclaim, and salvage. A kind of lyric scrapbook with pressed memories of quirky characters and outrageous incidents coming to life with each turned page, *The Silence of Red Glass* is rooted in a distinct Italian-American community. However, Wagner's vision branches out from that childhood into wide-angle elegies for coral reefs and wrens and the other harbingers of natural rhythms that slip like a word for that thing over there we can't quite name anymore. But buck up and dry your eyes, these poems also insist, the past isn't all past. We live in a world where there are planarian flat worms who can survive with memories intact even when cut into 300 pieces and it will take more than a sturdy shovel to stop those lily-of-the-valleys from coming back every year to take over the flower bed. We live in a world that once held Aunt Mary and we may yet grow into her legacy. *The Silence of Red Glass* is a book of poems that teaches us how to remember, how to grieve, and how to face the future with sturdy resolve.

Kathryn Nuernberger,
author of *The End of Pink*

Of *The Immigrants' New Camera*

Reading *The Immigrants' New Camera: A Family Collection* is like sitting down to a large Italian meal. Maryfrances Wagner's images are seasoned with the immediacy of Kansas City's Little Italy, the family kitchen, the table with its stories, tender, painful, and humorous. The poet's narratives simmer in the richness of the Italian-American experience. Yet, as the best poems do, Wagner's poetry connects the reader to the universal, but with a hint of fresh basil and chopped tomatoes.

Al Ortolani,
author of *On the Chicopee Spur*

Maryfrances Wagner's poetic gift is one that captures still moments overlooked in the spinning whirl of life. In this sensory album of autobiographical poems, many new, but the majority collected from previous books over the years, melodious rhythms sing through the pages, never failing to enchant. Wagner writes of people she has loved as family her whole life with delicate, layered imagery that evokes a mid-century mix of beauty and humor.

> Catherine Anderson,
> author of *Woman with a Gambling Mania*

The Immigrants' New Camera:
A Family Collection

Poems by Maryfrances Wagner

Kansas City Spartan Press Missouri

Spartan Press
Kansas City, Missouri
spartanpresskc.com

Copyright (c) Maryfrances Wagner, 2018
First Edition 1 3 5 7 9 10 8 6 4 2
ISBN: 978-1-946642-70-7
LCCN: 2018956808

Design, edits and layout: Jason Ryberg,
Cover art and design: Greg Field
Title page image: Greg Field
Author photo: Andrea Brookhart
All rights reserved. No part of this publication may be
reproduced or transmitted in any form or by any means,
electronic or mechanical, including photocopying,
recording or by info retrieval system, without prior
written permission from the author.

Spartan Press would like to thank Prospero's Books,
The Fellowship of N-finite Jest, The Prospero Institute
of Disquieted P/o/e/t/i/c/s, Will Leathem, Tom Wayne,
Jeanette Powers, j. d. tulloch, Jon Bidwell, Jason Preu,
Mark McClane, Tony Hayden and the whole Osage Arts
Community.

Acknowledgments:

Thanks to the magazines, anthologies, newspapers, and textbooks where these poems first appeared, sometimes in a slightly different version: Birmingham Poetry Review, Imagination & Place, Laurel Review, New Letters, Voices in Italian Americana, Any Key Press, Beacon Review, Envy's Sting, Nebraska Review, Jam Today, Midwest Quarterly, Karamu, Hiram Poetry Review, Integrity, Caprice, Kansas Quarterly, Cape Rock, Sing Heavenly Muse, Coal City Review, I-70 Review, Kansas City Voices, Louisville Review, Medulla Review, New Mexico Review, Poetry East, Patterson Literary Review, Potpourri, Stone Mountain Highway, Potpourri, Thorny Locust, MidAmerica Poetry Review, Red River Review, Rockhurst Review, The Same, Avocet, Chariton Review, Downgo Sun, Flint Hills Review, Chiron Review, Green Hills Literary Lantern, Rusty Truck, Dying Dahlia Review, Wild Goose Poetry Review, San Pedro River Review, Blue Unicorn, Mojave River Review, River City, Paddock Review, Poem, Bridge Eight, Eunoia Review, Connecticut River Review, Houseboat, Concho Review, Republish, Integrity, Tipton Literary Journal, Zingara, Amaryllis, The Kansas City Star, Pitch Weekly, Poets at Large (Helicon Nine), Bearing Witness: Poetry by Teachers about Teaching (Chicago Review), Chance of a Ghost (Helicon Nine), The Dream Book: An Anthology of Writings by Italian American Women (Syracuse), Literature Across Cultures (Pearson/Longman), Whirlybird Anthology of Greater Kansas City Poets (Whirlybird), Unsettling America: An Anthology of Contemporary Multicultural Poetry (Penguin), Avenues into Another Millennium: A Missouri Anthology (Sheba), Anthology of Missouri Women Writers (Sheba), Kansas City Outloud II (BkMk), Memories and Memoirs: An Anthology of Contemporary Missouri Writers (Sheba).

Thanks to BkMk, MidAm, Mammoth, Woodley, and Finishing Line presses where many of these poems appeared in the books *Bandaged Watermelons and Other Rusty Ducks, Tonight Cicadas Sing, Salvatore's Daughter, Red Silk, Light Subtracts Itself, Dioramas, The Silence of Red Glass,* and *Pouf.*

Special thanks to those who help us along the way. I can't imagine what I would do without them. So many parts go into the making of a book, and so many help along that way. Special thanks to the past press editors for publishing my books, and in the case of this new collection, many thanks to Jason Ryberg and Spartan Press.

Grateful thanks to Lola Haskins for her keen observations and helpful advice throughout the making of this collection, and thanks to Gay Dust and Jo McDougall for their advice and proofreading skills. Thanks to Catherine Anderson, Greg Field, and Al Ortolani for looking over the manuscript, and thanks to William Trowbridge, Gary Gildner, Alarie Tennille, Lindsey Martin-Bowen, Kathryn Nurenberger, Denise Low and Tina Hacker for their continued support.

For all of my Cusumano and Passiglia Famiglia

To my Cusumano storytellers: Zia Josie, Zia Gina, Zia Lena, Zia Sadie, Zia Rosie, Zia Martha, Zio Jasper, Zio Phil, Zio Nene, my father, Salvatore, and my many cugini still trying to help sort our stories we heard in varying versions

To my Passiglia storytellers: Uncle Carl Passiglia, Aunt Mary Frances Passiglia Balestrere, Cugino Jimmy Balestrere, and my mother, Marguerite Passiglia Cusumano

and for Greg Field, my dear husband, soul mate, and fellow traveler

TABLE OF CONTENTS

I

Uprooted / 1

What the Zie Told Us / 2

The Immigrants Get a New Camera / 4

Demoni / 5

Zia Rosie Talks About the Family Farm / 7

Zia Martha Talks About Open Air / 9

Zia Rosie Talks About Sundays / 10

Zia Martha Talks About Wanting a Car / 11

Zia Rosie Tells Us About the Thirties Sugar Houses / 12

Zia Rosie Tells the Story of Nonno's Death / 14

II

Neighborhood / 16

My Mother's White Lies / 17

Their Closets / 19

Photograph / 21

Miss Clement's Second Grade / 22

Hugging Mother / 23

My Brother's Room / 24

Magic Feet / 26

Chicks / 27

Joe / 29

Bringing Someone Home / 31

Lessons / 32

Learning to Be Small / 34

Furnace Room Escape / 35

Delphia in 4th Grade / 37

Aunt Mary Introduces Me to Peppers / 39

Aunt Mary Talks About Tony Fie / 41

Aunt Mary Explains White and Black Lies / 43

Aunt Mary Talks About Nonna / 45

Aunt Mary Shows Me How to Bake / 47

Where's Anthony / 49

Flight / 50

III

Outcasts / 52

First Days / 54

Raising a Hand / 55

Missouri Fig Trees / 56

Point of View / 57

Wishbone / 58

Strangers at the Table / 59

Hands / 60

Backyard Wishing Well / 61

Deer Hunting / 62

Bringing Home the Wild / 63

Sweatshirt Dress / 65

Crush on the Americano / 67

Ragazza / 69

Control / 70

Under the Table / 71

Preparations for an Italian Wedding / 73

IV

Victims Lose Direction / 76

Red Silk / 78

Wedding Night / 80

First Month / 82

Faces / 83

Ambush / 85

Separation / 86

Ghost in Starlight / 88

V

All The Time Running / 91

Rain Elegy / 92

After Signing Releases / 93

Chemotherapy / 94

Twelve Days on Methadone / 96

Giant Clown / 100

Margaret's Song / 102

The Importance of Kneading / 103

The Occasional Family / 105

Procession / 107

VI

Sorting Things Out / 109

My Father's Nightstand / 110

Winemaking / 111

Estate Sale / 113
The House / 114
Tuberoses / 116
Salute / 119
In a Season of Absence / 121

VII
New Starts / 123
Between Truth and Wish / 125
Beyond a Window of Light / 127
Scimeca's / 128
When I Am in My Kitchen / 129
Zia Rosie Lies Down with the Facts / 130
The Last Shot / 132
At the End / 134

VIII
Aunt Mary Postulates One Sunday
   at the Nursing Home / 137
I Bring Aunt Mary a Christmas Tree / 138
Aunt Mary Wants a Chef / 140
Aunt Mary Complains About Entertainment / 141
Aunt Mary Looks for Company / 142
Aunt Mary Wonders About Guests in the Hall / 143
Aunt Mary Pines for Shopping / 145
Aunt Mary Reflects on Her Passing / 146
Mantiglia / 148

IX

In Your Own Way / 150

Depth Finder / 151

Second Chance / 152

The Black-dress Ladies Sit Down with the Cousins
at Our Last Uncle's Wake / 154

Finding a Photo in the Attic / 156

Walking Sticks / 158

Don't Read in the Dark / 159

Black Bird / 161

Gifts / 163

Month of Ashes / 164

Illusions / 166

Glossary of Italian Words / 168

I

A trail of crumbs neither wind nor time can touch

Uprooted

Urban renewal bulldozed our first apartment
in the neighborhood where fathers worked

three jobs and mothers stoked furnaces
and stretched soup with tubettini and lentils.

The city built a hospital, torn down years later
to build an apartment complex for townies.

How deep down are the tin pails or silken baby shoes?
Every trip through the city, we stare at vacant

lots where we ate marshmallow sundaes and Dots,
where the deli wrapped our salami and Swiss

in white paper taped shut. We will always look
for traces: cup handle, glass knob, pocked pan—

or caved in soil exposing basement steps. They will
lead us back to crates of empty bottles and papers saved

from the old country in a language we can't speak.
A trail of crumbs neither wind nor time can touch.

What the Zie Told Us

I.

We *cugini* circled the *zie* at reunions
to hear their stories, our plates heaped
with rigatoni, eggplant, olives, bread.

The *zie* now dead, we sit at the table,
munch biscotti, sip anisette, jigsaw stories together
from versions we each know.

We imagine details: our nonno we never met
saw Maria, the blonde girl sniffing sage
in a Bivona market, her herbs for sale in baskets.

We guess he thought about her tiny hands
while staring at the moon above the Cianciano
mountains, his sheep huddled, his dogs watchful.

We know he borrowed a horse for the two-day ride.
Perhaps he rehearsed, knowing her father would say,
Come back when she's fifteen. The *zie* told us this.

Antonio did not leave. He took her back to Cianciano.
He saved. Our four zie born there only remember
sheep wool, basil in windows, and sea salt.

II.

Nonna Maria did not leave us her wisdom of herbs.
She fumbled with English as if each word were a chalkboard
problem she couldn't solve. The language of her hands

urgent but beyond us, we hugged her, accepted her *biscotti*
shaped like birds, listened to our parents talk to her in
Italian we never learned. We pass around our photo of her

wearing a straw hat. She stood beside the *S.S. Germania*
at Ellis Island, four daughters wrapped around her.
They all wore the look that comes before knowing, like iris

breaking through snow— long before losing Nonno Antonio,
before us. From our mothers we learned to bake, to use
rosemary, oregano. Around the table, we guess she wore

daisies in her hair at the wedding, guess papa slicked
back his hair. We clink glasses, *salute,* toast our seasoned
stories with our poor handful of Italian words.

The Immigrants Get a New Camera

No one knew when they stood on Stanley Hill,
each waiting to hold the new family camera.
They didn't mind sharing among the eleven of them,
one capturing the bridge over the north end, another
the city skyline, the old airport. Sadie took candids
of Josie scratching her bites, Lena hiking up her
sagging skirt. Sam lined up Gene and Phil saluting,
Jay making a pig face, Nene showing his new tooth
coming in, all of them in costumes they'd found
at the dump. It was all about holding the black box
for the first time, framing those frozen moments
before listening for the lever's click. Frank snapped
Rosie singing *The Continental* while she swished
the yellow skirt of her dance hall costume,
little Martha imitating her sister's swing,
Nene turning somersaults down the hill.
No one knew they couldn't afford film.

Demoni

Demons haunted the house
on Camel Street, made Papa
drop his fork, wave his shotgun.
The children huddled under the table.

One Christmas, *demoni*
let a pig in to root through
wrapped yo-yos and knitted sweaters.
Shivering under blankets,
Sadie and Lena heard them
on the steps, heard glass
hit the fireplace.
Basta, Nonna said. *No more
trees, no wrapped presenti.
Now on, peanuts and oranges.*

The next fall, Martha asked nightly
for a doll. No *store bambola,*
Papa said and whittled her a horse.
Rosie sharpened a pencil,
wrote Tom Pendergast:
*If you care so much
about the poveri, then
buy my sister a doll.*

On Christmas Eve, the *bambola*
arrived in silver paper.
Papa set down his carved sheep,
his crate of oranges.
Nonna crossed herself,
whispered, *Demoni*.
Rosie and Martha twirled,
then sharpened another pencil.

Zia Rosie Talks About the Family Farm

We never knew we were poor. Always plenty to eat. Had two cows named Bay and Rosie. We used to squirt each other with the milk. Your father and Jay pulled a calf out of Rosie's stomach once. Martha and I scooted around to watch behind the fence. The calf came out the wrong way. It was already dead, and the cow was in so much pain. It kept ooooohhhh hing. Nonna made ricotta and mozzarella with the milk. We had goats too, and sometimes Papa killed a goat. He'd get a stick to pull the skin off. After he killed it, he tied it up and plunged a dagger in its neck and prayed and prayed. The blood poured out into a bucket. He put the stick up through the foot and worked off the hide. The stick had a hole in it so he could blow air and make the skin swell. Then he could pull it off. If you didn't do it right, it ruined the meat. People always wanted to buy half a goat at Easter. Gina always said she didn't want to eat any goat, but at dinner, she always ate the most. Papa also sheared sheep, and your dad held the sheep down while Papa sheared them. Wool popped out all over. Nonna washed the fleece and stuffed the mattresses with it. It got knotty, but she'd pull it back apart and fluff it up. She made blankets out of the wool. Before he married Nonna, Papa herded sheep. They both wanted lots of children. Nonna was 44 when she had Aunt Martha, and if nothing had happened to Papa, they wanted even more. We think she had fifteen, and at least two died in Italy. A son named Diaspro and a girl named Rosa. Guess they wanted kids with those names because they used them again. We knew two died here, one an infant and one at three, and then we lost Frank in a car accident when he was eighteen. That left ten of us. Still a bunch of us sitting at the dinner table every night.

Zia Martha Talks About Open Air

We lived next door to an Ethiopian family, and the sister we played with had tuberculosis. Since we hung out with them, the school thought we probably had it too, so they put us in Open Air. That's what they called it. Open Air. They did this for kids they thought were sickly. We spent an hour in the morning and an hour in the afternoon outside. We had class in the morning. Mostly history. They talked about Germany and building up arms. Sometimes the girls learned a little sewing. I made an apron. At noon, they fed us something they thought was nourishing — usually milk and bread with sauerkraut or tomato soup. In the afternoon, they made us lie down on cots in the sun. I hated that food they gave us, and I kept telling them we had plenty to eat at home, but Uncle Nene always told me to hush. He loved that tomato soup. He gobbled his up. Then he ate mine, and sometimes Rosie's, but Uncle Nene would eat anything. He didn't care. He told everyone, *Give me what you don't want.*

Zia Rosie Talks About Sundays

We were always good kids. We never did anything violent or vicious. We all got a nickel on Sunday to spend after church. Mama always said, *You want to go to the show, but you better not go to the show. Your eyes are gonna get full, but your stomach will be empty. Go buy a pie instead.* Mama loved candy and fried pies, and she bought big hunks of chocolate and pink and white marshmallow cookies covered in coconut. So, we bought a pie or candy and tried to sneak into the show, but that almost never worked. One of us would pay and go in and then open the back door for the rest of us, but the girl who worked there and took the money watched us. She knew we were up to something. By then several of us were married, but everyone came home on Sunday afternoon. We always had meatballs, stuffed peppers, stuffed eggplant and *sugo*. Sometimes stuffed pasta. That was our night meal, and most of the time Papa made ice cream with peanuts in it.

Zia Martha Talks About Wanting a Car

I wasn't the only one asking when we were going to
get a car. Rosie, Sadie, and Gina did too. We had a
horse and a wagon, but after we moved into the North
End, we really needed a car to get around. Finally,
Papa said, *Come on over here, and I'll show you
when.* He held his cupped hand open and said, *When
hair starts to grow in here. You see any hair?*
We shook our heads, but we kept asking him every
week if any hair started growing yet. We never did
get a car.

Zia Rosie Tells Us
About The Thirties Sugar Houses

They were on every corner.
Got sugar from one man.
The Greigos next door had a still.
I could breathe fumes, houses
so close they couldn't sag, windows
so near we could see each other scratch.
They passed sacks through our window.
They told Nonna it was easier that way.

Sometimes they gave her a little whiskey
leftover in the barrel. She filled
tiny bottles and took nips
when she needed a little pepping up,
good medicine for the right thing.

Some of them went to jail.
Miss Maddie. They caught her.
She was in a cell with *puttani*.
They felt her hair, breathed down
her neck, told her she smelled sweet.
She said, *Say another word, I'm gonna
let you have it!* as if five-foot Ms. Maddie
ever let anybody have anything, even a sip.
They left her alone and went to prison.
Miss Maddie must've known somebody.
She came home. *A little pazza. Fortunato.*

Nene found liquor hidden in tunnels
under the street on Forest, where dirt
caved in on an empty lot. He saw skeletons
in baskets, naked women painted on walls.

The big shots lived on Quality Hill then,
but everybody went down to the speakeasies
to drink and *danza*. The big shots had
nice houses, but drunks and the homeless

fell off Cliff Drive or through the hill cracks.
Funeral-home nets fished them into baskets
long after they were dead. Found them by smell.
Back then, almost anything was okay.
People really dressed. Lots'a people'd
like to see it that way again.

Zia Rosie Tells the Story of Nonno's Death

We were walking home from church on a Sunday night
with Papa Antonio, the nonno you cugini never met.
Papa was dancing in the spirit, and Zio Alex was singing
with Zia Martha when two men ran from a North End
saloon shooting at each other, so drunk their aim was off.
I saw the sparks in the dark. Zio Alex shielded us and
said to run home. He threw himself on his Papa and
sobbed. Blood streamed down the curb. A policeman
came out of the bar carrying a pint he stuffed in his jacket.
I was nine, but I remember. I wouldn't leave the house.
Afraid to play. Threw up for days. You think you can
depend on some things like the moon in the sky and
dinner with your family. Most of us were still kids. Nothing
was ever going to be the same. I'd never see Papa carrying
home the biggest turkey for Christmas or Sundays when he
made ice cream with peanuts we shelled after church. Your
father had to leave college to help take care of us. Nonna
Maria dyed seven dresses black. Our cugini brought
lasagna, *biscotti,* Anisette, oranges, sat up with us for three
nights. We took turns taking naps. Fifteen years later, the
police wanted Zio Alex to identify the men in a lineup.
Too late by then. Too late as soon as those men came out
of that bar.

II

I watch myself watching myself watch

Neighborhood

Of our first house, only pictures remain.
My babysitter holding me, we smile
from three wooden steps
where Phyllis poked Frank's eyes
with her baton.
In another, my brother
shrugs against a table,
clean as every room is clean
like a tucked fresh sheet.
Mother scooped coal in that basement,
her nightgown hidden by her coat,
while my father rewired buildings at night
so the dentist's chair gleamed with light,
and the lawyers' cigars' fat ashes
disappeared with swept shavings.
Now a medical center closes us out
of the block where we ran in tidy yards,
only an easement like a seam
separating one kitchen from another.
The porch where we stuffed grasshoppers
between cracks
is a hospital room now.
On the street where we once belonged,
an IV hangs from its silver pole.

My Mother's White Lies

If you don't fall asleep during your nap by four o'clock,
        you'll get polio.
        Then you'll have to live
        in a big iron tank for the rest
        of your short life.

If you giggle like that much longer,
        you'll get worms. They'll crawl
        all through your body and come out
        at night to look at you while you sleep.

If you aren't asleep when Santa comes,
        he puts all of your presents back
        in his bag and marks an X on the roof.
        Then he never brings any more presents.

Don't you ever get up at night and wander
        outside. The Boogey Man waits out there
        for small children and eats their souls.
        You can't get into heaven without a soul.

See, every time you fall down like that,
        it's for something you did wrong—
        like not telling me the truth. God punishes,
        and he sees all those things
        you aren't telling me about.

If you run through the house or climb
        into that attic, the Big Bad Wolf
        who ate Red Riding Hood's nonna
        will come out from hiding in the rafters,
        and you can figure out the rest.

If you go in the water sooner than an hour after you eat,
        you'll sink to the bottom and drown, and if
        you have on one of those bikini tops, it will
        come loose, and the lifeguard will find you
        half naked when he brings you out,
        and everyone will see.

Don't ever let anybody touch you down there
        until you're married. No boy will want you
        after that because you won't be a virgin.
        Boys only marry virgins. You'd have to wait
        for a widower. They don't care so much.

Don't sit out there in the driveway after you
        get home from a date. Remember, I'm watching
        from the window, but the neighbors will see too.
        It will ruin your reputation forever.
        They'll tell everyone.

Their Closets

I. Nonno

Each Monday, eight shirts,
clung to puffed hangers.
Fine cotton, loose

monogrammed bodies,
unwrinkled tails, stiff collars
pressed down tight and straight.

Nonno's eight winter, long-sleeved,
then eight summer short-sleeved,
perfectly aligned beside

eight tailored suits. Six hats
on the closet shelf waiting
for their season. So much space,

so much room for three
pairs of shoes. In his dresser,
a dozen, folded t-shirts,

Boy Scout shirt, Scoutmaster
shirt. A dozen black,
a dozen white socks,

line up like soldiers curled
in small spaces, all trained,
hunchbacked, and trenched.

II. Nonna

At the back of her double-wide
walk-in, her leftovers

sprawl in woven baskets
near next season's moth-proofed

and wrapped mink coat. On long racks,
dresses smash against each other.

Scarves stream from hooks, puddle
on the floor. Stacked hatboxes

tip their lids from untied strings.
Sequined and sleek gowns hover

above stacks of shoes nowhere near mates.
Drawers spill their bra straps and tatted collars.

Silk stockings dangle from knobs. Garters
and hair ribbons drape over Woolf's and Hall's

sacks of gloves, satin pajamas and lacy nightgowns
still snug in their cellophane packages.

Photograph

I took them from the attic suitcase
of Nonna's snapshots,
a black and white past
of cross-armed uncles leaning against roadsters,
cousins sucking in pasta,
Bisnonna in the fields of Bivona,
Nonno laying peonies over gravestones—
faces before I was born.
In this shot, Nonna stands beside a Pieta,
one hand clutching an alligator bag,
one hand over her heart,
alone with God at Capistrano.
When I stayed with her,
she clicked rosary beads,
eyes half mast, silk stockings rolled to ankles,
her lips shaping words she never shared.
After she knelt for prayers at bedtime,
she turned down our blankets,
said good night to Nonno,
who slept in his own bed,
then climbed between pink satin sheets,
alone, as she always was with God.

Miss Clement's Second Grade

We sat in even rows
like new chocolates in a long box,
quiet enough to hear pencils
trying uneven letters.

On those days I stared
at clean blue-lined paper
while boiler heat sifted
through thumping registers
by Anthony's desk.

I shaped vowels,
and wished I were a Smith
so I could hand out crayons,
have my papers on display.

During quiet writing,
when everyone seemed the same,
I almost forgot
the hours Miss Clement
locked me in the closet.

Every day she wore a navy dress,
tied her blond hair in a circular braid.

Every night I laughed
with Wilbur and Charlotte.
They didn't mind my Italian name.

Hugging Mother

I slouched against her,
sagged into her skirt folds
to hide from strangers or uncles
who rubbed whiskers on my cheeks.

I leaned into her shirtwaists
to hide a missing tooth,
a broken nose, a line of stitches
across my forehead.

On bus rides, I huddled under her arm
and listened to the hiss of the bus door,
the judder of the steering wheel,
the pop of gum, until the trees blurred
and my eyelids surrendered.

My Brother's Room

The Vargas playing cards lounged on his dresser
where anyone could find them.
By the time I was seven, I had combed
his room daily for licorice, Juicy Fruit gum,
and the unfamiliar. I read his pirate
paperbacks, examined whatever he
left out: emerald cuff links, ticket stubs,
glass bowl of trinkets, a girl's earring.
I wondered where he went every night
in a clean shirt my mother pressed.
Stay out of my room, he said. *Nothing in here
for you to see.* Ten years older, he was choosing
colleges with swimming scholarships
and getting calls from girls he met at dances.
I still dressed paper dolls and drew on a magic window.
The deck of Vargas cards was not like the ones
my parents used when they played pinochle.
On every card, a see-through body stocking,
negligee, or skimpy swimsuit barely covered
a shapely woman, some wearing little more
than a big hat and high heels. Some held props –
a teacup, an umbrella, a pumpkin, a bow and arrow.
I sorted them side-by-side on his bed, getting an idea
of how men expected women to look.
My mother found me and shooed me out.
You know your brother doesn't want you in here.

The next day when I foraged, the Vargas girls
were gone, but I found a folded packet
and opened it. When my mother appeared, I held it up,
Look! Look at this little white balloon.

Magic Feet

When he failed chemistry,
spent grocery money on comic books,
broke his retainer again, my mother chased
my brother Anthony around the table, yardstick,
a foil plunging after him.
He always joked her into a good laugh,
and she never delivered a blow.
Somehow they ended up dancing,
a tango down the hall, a fox trot in the kitchen.
Sometimes they shoved table against window,
stacked chairs, rolled up the rug, and dragged
out 45's. There on her prized parquets,
waxed too often, buffed every week,
they danced, sock footed, their sidekicks
and twirls digging into that shine.
Her shirtwaist flounced and belled;
their arms waved above their heads.
He swung her over his back,
and she slid into the splits through his legs.
Hip bumpers, foot thumpers,
mother and son rocked until time to put supper on.
Furniture back in place,
report card, comic books, or retainer
waited on the table for Dad.

Chicks

Along the trail, I find a nest upside down
and four fallen eggs, speckled like seeded loaves.

I think about this beak and wing, one black eye, wet
dotted masses of possible feathers. Once my brother

gave me a dozen chicks for Easter. I named them
and strutted them around the porch until they

became hens and a rooster. Two wandered
under the railing, and then we had ten. The hens

laid eggs we ate for breakfast. The rooster
started crowing several times a day, sometimes

at three or six am. That final *errrr* floated
down the street and through the windows

of the Bakers, the Parkers, the Bells. They
wondered, called my mother, then together

called the mayor, who called us.
See what you've done, my mother told

my brother, then held the phone close
and whispered when she called my father.

He took them to our cousin's farm, a far-away,
third cousin I didn't know. I had failed

the chickens even though I slept on the porch
all summer to keep them safe. Mother said

the chickens would have more room
to strut, to live long lives, and she held

to the belief that they might live nearly forever
on a farm too far away for us to drive.

Joe

After my dad's hunting dogs,
my mother said, over and over,
No more pets, no more tracks,
no more clumps or floating hair.
I'd have to make do with Charlie,
Nonna's stray that lived under the porch
and let only Nonna touch him.

We settled on a parakeet I named Joe.
He learned to say *Hello* and *Pretty boy.*
He chirped and trilled and danced
across his perch. Sometimes my mother
propped open his cage with a hairpin
so he could air his wings and ride
on our shoulders or an extended finger.

When he hanged himself on the door wire,
we held a burial in the backyard. After
I sat quietly for days, Joe started coming
around in the afternoons to help me
dust or make sand cookies. Mother
set a place at the table for him, but he
never ate the cookies or the salad.

He disappeared long after I knew he
wasn't there, and sometimes my mother
and I sat at the table in quiet and stared
out the window where so many birds
explored the houses she hung outside.

Bringing Someone Home

Leonard always threw rocks to make his point.
He once gashed open David's head because rather
than climb on the American Legion roof, David
wanted to go to Lou's for a marshmallow sundae.
Leonard was always out stabbing mice or
smashing bottles, trying to find players for
Truth or Dare. We learned that game always meant
someone took his pants down or went home bleeding.
He let Jimmy off once, allowing him to eat
a cigarette rather than a beetle. Once, he set
Billy Martin's cat on fire to see what would happen.
When Karen Nash promised to tell he'd killed a cat,
Leonard said he didn't have a damn mom. I
followed him home to see for myself.
Home was a garage below a boarding house.
A long extension cord through the ceiling
provided their only light. Leonard brought water
from a common bathroom upstairs to offer me a drink.
A spoon in a can of Strongheart waited on the table
to feed a hunger sharper than a blade edge. I kept staring
at his father standing in boxer shorts, a single bulb
haloing a bottle in one hand as he lashed his belt
at Leonard with the other for bringing someone home.

Lessons

> *Children should be seen, not heard.* ~ Mirk's Festial

I hide in Nonna's bedroom closet,
past winter's nubby sweaters,
past hem-torn drapes
where she can't find me.
I fold myself into a basket,
a blanket over me, quiet,
as the child combing pink doll hair,
while Nonna kneels into prayers,
her fingers finding each bead;
quiet, as the child sitting
while Nonna snips rosemary
and basil into a garlicky red sauce,
quiet, as the child Nonna teaches
to roll transparent dough, to loop
yarn through a hook over and over
until the room feels as heavy
as wet wool and dark silence.

Nonna taught me to push back
words that try for speech
from the throat's darkest basement.
The child who learned to be quiet
isn't saying, *Here, here I am*
when Nonna calls. Not enough
to have an unfindable place.

I don't save her from poking under beds,
from shuttling outside, sandbox to bushes,
her call more and more broken, *Dove sei,
Beata Madre, where are you?*
I creep from closet to couch,
wait, and perfect French knots
on a pillowcase for my hope chest,
needle through cloth the only sound.

Learning to Be Small

In my corner of our hallway,
I take tea with Alice and Mad Hatter.

Here's my royal towel-cape,
my small altar where I hear

the prayer of *Shhhhhh,*
where I wait to be spoken to,

to be blessed with bonbons
for being a quiet girl.

I imagine myself
a molecule, snow falling.

I know not to jump or wiggle.
I don't fidget when I brood.

I tuck into chairs, a mannequin,
my hands two lap rocks.

I don't run through houses,
scratch floors, blow whistles, shriek.

I know laughter will give me worms.
I am a child mime:

I watch myself
watching myself watch.

Furnace Room Escape

Its eight arms stretch
across the room, its face

the cast-iron furnace door,
crooked and slightly ajar.

Flames I fear shift
and arc from that core.

Coals breathe red then shed
gray-blue ash through a grate.

At eight, I see its rage
each time it roars back on—

its flames dancing devils,
in the room I always sneak past.

On this winter day, the furnace
becomes a womb, a respite

from my mother's pursuit
with raised broom.

I don't remember what I did
that would stoke such wrath.

I run into the furnace room
to hide behind its arms,

into a nook she can't reach.
She thrashes at me as if I am

a moth, a black widow, a rat,
her arms as persistent as the flames.

Delphia in 4th Grade

She skidded us off our feet in dodgeball,
sent Bobby Shad sliding across the circle,
sailed all kicked balls past reaching arms.

Six girls followed her around like good
Davidians armed with long nails.
First year of integration at Linwood.

Before, I had reigned as the outcast Italian
kicker. The day I called her Philadelphia,
she gored me with her eyes. As we sanded

blocks for the Fort Osage replica, Bobby said,
Philadelphia has good sanding rhythm. She
spun around, smacked his fingers with her block,

and snapped, *Don't call me Philadelphia.* Bobby
crept to another table. *He's only being friendly,*
I said. She was waiting after school.

Could've laid me out with one swing. *Where
you going? Why'd you defend that little twerp?*
She clicked her long red nails, hissed, *At kickball,*

you smacked a home run. Lucky, I shrugged. She
pinched my arm. *Well, it's my game.* Six girls
moved in and narrowed their eyes. I raised

a hand. Delphia dug a pencil into my wrist
and scraped under my arm with her nails. *Don't
call me Philadelphia, and don't kick like that*

unless you're on my team. They chuckled off, clicking
their weapons. My mother blotted me with iodine,
but the infection lasted through six weeks of penicillin.

After that, if we played kickball and I didn't end up
on her team, I faked a twisted ankle, allergies,
some reason to go back to the classroom and read.

Aunt Mary Introduces Me to Peppers

Come out here on the porch.   We can enjoy the breeze.
Feel it? *Bello.* I love it out here. Besides, I passed

the Hoover and don't want anyone walking on the floor.
Not even barefoot. Jimmy always gets the honor

of pulling the plug out. I'm afraid I'll get shocked, but he
never does. You want a Coke? I'm gonna have one. Let's

get some crackers and olives and peppers, but you can't
have the peppers. *Caldo.* Too hot. Help me bring it out.

This mozzarella is fresh from Scimeca's today. Nonna
made it better. Little basil and tomato. *Oh mio.*

Oh, for some of her *pane* and that good butter Newtie
gets at the city market. Uncle Johnny brought salami

and prosciutto too, and those snails that wiggle
in wire baskets. I'm not touching anything that moves.

Uncle Johnny can make that dish that sounds like eggs
in a cart with a little go at the end. Not me. Scimeca's has

good sausage too— not as good as Jenny's husband makes
for their restaurant. I'm putting sausage in Sunday's *sugo.*

Leave those peppers alone. *Basta!* I'm telling you they're hot. They'd burn your throat. Maybe when you're twenty you can

try them. Or if your mother decides to give you one. Have some salami. The black pepper in there will be hot enough.

And here's a little celery. It's good with cheese. We have ourselves a little feast. Uncle Johnny'll be here soon.

He'll make us a whisky highball. You can have another Coke. See Nonna's cat Charlie down there watching birds? He's

sneaky. *Subdolo.* I've seen him catch mice and sparrows. Mostly he sleeps in the basement and waits for something

to move. *Pigro gatto.* There you go again. Got your hand on a pepper. Okay, go on. Do it. See for yourself. Don't tell

your mother it was my idea. Uh huh, I know you're acting like you like them, but I see tears, and you can't catch

your breath. Here, drink your Coke. It'll help, but don't blame me. I warned you. Try again when you're older.

You're nothing like Jimmy. He listens. You? *Testa dura.* I got a feeling that's how you're going to learn a lot of things.

Aunt Mary Talks about Tony Fie

I never understood why Toni Fie came around—
unless it was to mooch off your mother and Nonna.

None of us really knew much about him, but he
was one *brutta faccia*. *Brutta, brutta* — and strange.

Even Jimmy thinks Tony Fie is strange. Comes around
when the men are gone to con Nonna or your mother

out of food — or if he needs your dad to fix something.
We don't know where he lives or what he does.

Maybe Nonno knows. Maybe Nonno helps him out.
Maybe he's homeless. Musta had a bad life from his looks.

If he is homeless, that's not *buffo*. In that case, I'm sorry
for him. Not knowing his past doesn't make him evil, but

he speeds down Linwood on that clattery motorcycle, half
the time with that mangy cat in his sidecar. He looks like

Mr. Magoo in thick-lens goggles and an aviator cap. Your
mother gives him Manor Man cinnamon rolls or her pie.

Never knew what he wanted from Nonna, but he always
starts with her. Mostly, she shoos him off like a sewer rat.

Sometimes he must say the magic word, and she fills a
big sack. Not much room left in the sidecar for the cat.

I never answer the door when he knocks. I don't want him
coming into my kitchen. He's one big *chiaccierone*. Always

telling stories. Most of them *bugie*. Big lies. Talks and talks
about nothing. *Niente*. Takes forever before he leaves.

He floats Sen Sens on his tongue and grins when he gossips
about Louie Valenti's mistress or Marie Casconi's facelift —

as if he knew either one of them. How does he know stuff?
He smells too. Like *alito cattivo*, wet wool and anise. I turn

away when he smiles. Green flecks in the few teeth he has.
The rest of his mouth looks like a bunch of Blackjack gum.

Musta had the pox. His face looks hail-damaged. To this
day I don't know how he knows us. *Mistero*. I wonder

if he drops in on other people. *Grande mistero*. Never know,
though. A good man can be disguised as a beast.

Aunt Mary Explains White and Black Lies

If your mother said you'd get worms
if you laughed too much, I'm not saying

otherwise. She's your mother. Talk to her.
It's more believable than what Nonna told us.

They believed strange things in the old country,
but Nonna never followed her own advice.

When she went to Vegas all alone, I knew she
cranked slot machines all day instead of praying

with Sisters of the Poor. Couldn't lift her suitcase
with those silver dollars weighing it down.

She had a nice photo to wave at Nonno of her
standing in front of the Church with the Sisters.

Fortunately, Nonno didn't notice the new Prada bag
on her arm or those sexy open-toed heels

he didn't like. Maybe he knew. Never said much.
She couldn't lie, though, about sideswiping

Louie Tamino's car with that long stripe of red paint
on her white and turquoise fender. When she lied

about eating one bite from all of the Russell Stover
box of chocolates or taking the biggest artichoke

because the bottom was burned, she called them
white lies, *bugie bianche,* lies that didn't hurt anybody —

like when I tell Uncle Johnny I only paid
twenty dollars for this skirt, or if

Angie Spalitto asks if she looks like a *puttana*
in her tight, red cocktail dress.

I've seen your mother lie. No one can
bring home twenty sacks of Price candy

and say it cost only two dollars. You gotta be
careful, though. You could go to prison for some lies.

You can't say you didn't sock someone if the next day
his eye turns purple and his lip swells. You could say

someone else did it, but you'd know it was a lie.
You'd feel it right in here. Those are black lies.

You want to stay away from that kind of lie.

Aunt Mary Talks About Nonna

I know your Nonna loved *As the World Turns*
and *Guiding Light*. Watched them every day,

but twice a day you had to get quieter than a dustball
when she said her rosary, every afternoon and evening.

You know what I'm saying. You've sat there in silence
with her while she does it. She wouldn't even let you

read or color. *Stare into space,* she always told you.
Before bed, she read from the prayer book by her

nightstand. So *religiosa*. Then she crossed herself
and lay under that sun lamp. To cool herself off,

she ate a pint of pineapple sherbet. It's a wonder such a
religious woman could live as she did. Nothing

stopped her. She thought enough time in confessional
took care of the *peccati*. She had proof. Calloused knees.

Grace, she said, *reaches us all. Chi lo sa?* Maybe she was
right. No wonder she had calluses. She asked for forgiveness

often enough. All that cheating at pinochle. If the dealer
dealt her too many nines, she'd throw the hand in,

say, *Misdeal.* Uncle Johnny and your Dad got so mad.
Any time she played bingo or any card game, she insisted

it had to be for money. Never played for fun. Even you kids
had to play for chocolates. Quite the gambler,

your Nonna. Went to Las Vegas every year by herself.
Drank lots of champagne, won her silver dollars, ate lobster.

You'd ask her what she did out there, and she'd put Mario Lanza
on the phonograph and drown you out. All those *white lies*

she told. You'd think people were out hitting her car
with bats and sideswiping her on purpose. Poor Nonno

never got an honest answer from her. She did her best to be
gone when there might be an issue to discuss. She had her ways.

Nonna had a good soul, though, and made time for all of the
bambini, took care of any of you if asked, even if you had to

watch Lawrence Welk or help her keep track of nine bingo cards.
After all, money was involved. More eyes helped. *Più gli occhi.*

Aunt Mary Shows Me How to Bake

You wanna make *biscotti* like your *zie*? Okay.
Va bene. Andiamo. You need a big bowl like this.

Sift in five pounds of flour. See? Sounds
like a lot. Don't worry. We always start

with five to make cookies for weddings
or the St. Joseph table. That's how Nonna

taught me and her mama taught her. How
Josephine Pisciotta and all the women bake

in the North End. Don't worry. They'll get
eaten. Always do. Feel that dip in your palm?

Fill that with baking powder. Toss it in. Pinch
of salt. Now, make a well. Fill it with eggs.

I don't know how many. Until it looks right.
Watch me. See, this full. *Guarda!* Count those.

That's how many. Splash of milk. Couple
handfuls of sugar. This much butter

but mostly Crisco. Big dollop. We can use
this cup if you want. It's about right. Be sure

it's more Crisco and not all butter like I know
you'll wanna do. It's about texture. *Struttura.*

After a few tries, you'll know what I'm saying.
Don't know why this is a surprise. Your mother

never measures. Doesn't even have measuring cups
or spoons. At least I have some somewhere.

Oh, and some vanilla. Real thing. When we
dye the icing, we'll add more flavors: anise, lemon,

you'll see. Right now, we got the dough. We'll make
different shapes, add pecans to some, *giugiulena,*

almonds. Right now, we'll put the dough
in the Frigidaire and bake them tomorrow.

I'm not up to all that rolling today.
How about some homemade cocoa—

none of those packets. While you drink it,
I'll make a pizza for dinner. I know it's 4:00,

but it'll be ready in a little over an hour.
I use Hot Roll mix. Shhh! Nobody can tell

the difference. Don't tell your mother or Aunt Sarah.
They waste a whole day making bread.

No one has to know. *Segreto.* We don't tell
all our secrets. Keep that in mind.

Where's Anthony?

Around the tube with popcorn and Coke,
we watch for my brother on *Arthur Murray*.
In daylight, he *finds himself by* changing majors:
engineering, visual arts, chemistry.
At night, he teaches dancing, glides partners
through tricky steps, makes them flow around him.

Watching, Mother and Aunt Mary jiggle to *Peggy Sue*,
while Nonna keeps asking, *Where's Anthony?*
Nonno's convinced a perfect samba
will not steer my brother toward the jewelry business,
but we all watch, even though Anthony's abandoned
anesthesiology and dentistry for tango.

As Dad raises a finger once more for education,
Arthur Murray whirls out, dipping Kathryn's arm
for the show's finale. The floor fills with waltzing couples.
We fall silent, eyes focused. In the screen's lower corner,
hair slicked, smiling in his tuxedo, Anthony flashes by.

Flight

Andrea Lang stepped into her father's Buick.
Her white angora tam framed her face, pink

and crowded as a rose. We didn't think it'd be
the last time we saw her or her perfectly formed

Palmer-method letters, her tight braids, her straight
teeth, her unscuffed pumps. On the playground

where she wouldn't kick a ball, she puffed her cheeks
and stood like someone lost in Paris.

In her tidy drawers, every sock was folded into
a suffocated calla lily. If one sagged or relaxed

out of form, she yanked them all out and started
again while her father watched approvingly.

He scolded her once for spilling baking soda
while he made brownies. Didn't she remember

how baking soda loses its lift if left out, didn't she,
didn't she remember? Into the Buick's leather seat,

she scooted, pulling her woolen Chanel skirt
over her knees, off to the better part of town.

III

We kept on wishing and tossing while the coins
arched and stacked and sank into the mud.

Outcasts

Theda's braids swished as she jumped
the double ropes of red hot peppers,
until she tangled and plunged under
a hail of jeers. She jumped longer,
faster, lived next door to Roger Maris,
but she was a new girl, like me.

Theda, squirming in a sixth-grade body,
her heart a question mark waiting
for a place to go, tugged her braids
across her eyes when Miss Penny
peered over reading glasses in search
of fraction sums. Beside her, I lined
my body exactly behind Bob Tackett,
my feet and hands still as coffins.
It was math. One of our names
would hobble out like a hunched troll.

Theda's voice wobbled forth a guess.
Yanked to the board for a second try,
she rubbed the chalk, pinched her lip,
and squeaked out another miss.

Miss Penny hiked Theda on a stool,
squeezed a dunce cap over her bangs,
and left her to burn and ascend while

the rest of us chanted capitals, located
Iowa and Alabama, cut ornaments for
our tree. I brushed Theda as I hung
my angel by the red light flashing on
her face like a siren, but she was already gone.

First Days

Slumped over in my back-row chair,
I sat every September, twisting my
ring around a moist finger, rolling
new pencils on my desk to air out
my hands, waiting, always waiting,
that pebble hardening in my throat.
Pat Adams, Billy Brown, easy names.
Only I made the teacher stumble,
four vowels clogging the tongue.
As the teacher waited, I repronounced
my name, my voice a wobbly pushcart
squeaking down the aisle, my hands
creeping up my face to cover a flush.
By Diane White and Dennis Yates,
I could swallow again.
After roll sheets and the inky scent
of new books lured me to Pharaohs,
pronouns or pie graphs, my feet
shuffled under my desk,
trying to find their place.

Raising a Hand

The teacher asks the meaning of a story. You
raise your hand. No one else does. The teacher

surveys the room, asks, *Doesn't anyone know
the answer?* Your hand flags the air. Heads

beside you stare at their desks. A few tap a finger
to a cheek, wait for an answer. Your hand

is a lone periscope. The teacher hunts. You
unzip your backpack, pull out a pencil, a black

marker and a sheet of paper, let your fingers
trace the page before you begin to draw

lines. Then doors. The teacher says, *Anyone
want to guess?* You've already gone through one

of the doors into a yard where a crow eyes a bit
of green glass, where insects click from trees,

where a hornworm, an egg sac on his back,
hollows and evaporates as baby spiders feed.

Missouri Fig Trees

In the Missouri soil
where his brother said
they'd never survive,
Salvatore hoed red clay clumps,
swore he'd make fig trees grow.
Every spring Salvatore loosened the soil,
pinched in peat and lime,
wore wheel tracks
from cowshed to garden,
hauling manure to once lean spindles,
now thick with new rings.
Some years he watered them from drought,
watched the ground swallow pools of water
purling through the hose.
Before frost, he bagged the trees,
tucked them under plastic, rugs, and wire.
They survived the snows;
they survived the ice storms.
They remind me of you, his brother said.
Now when tomatoes sag on vines,
Salvatore loads baskets
throbbing with heavy-bellied figs.

Point of View

My father hoisted me on his palm
until I was old enough to straddle
the twin bones of his shoulders.
From that view I was eye level
with Shriners tossing gumballs in parades,
beauty queens waving from floats.

He held me at the circus
to watch twenty clowns
exit a Volkswagen. We
lumbered as if on stilts.
I could see every kid below
jumping for a glance, every head
jockeying for an open space,

From the ground, I watched
between fence slats or nose
pressed into the thighs of a crowd.
Sometimes I pushed and elbowed
my way to a glimpse.

My father's shoulders provided
a stepladder to the possible,
past mowed fields,
past water towers and ponds,
the beyond within reach.

Wishbone

The wishes never came true,
but every Christmas
when the turkey was a dinasaurial hull,
and the wishbone had dried in the window,
out came the nutcrackers, Nonna's *pignolate*,
and Mother carrying the arched bone.
Who's gonna wish? she asked
looking down at her crew,
languid as arctic seals from Dad's anisette,
dozing in and out of hearing
how much we needed a white Christmas,
how much wild rice cost this year.
Needles, pins... she started us out,
Triplets, twins, Dad helped.
Sometimes the bone wasn't quite dry,
so greasy it frogkicked through fingers
right on Mother's brocade couch.
Some careless years, before Dad
could wave it like a crackerjack prize,
his grinning face gleaming with turkey scraps,
it broke under his knife.
When we asked why we had to wish,
Mother pinched fingers together,
punched them in the air.
You want no cannoli, no biscotti?
She gave us the look.
It worked on us every year.

Strangers at the Holiday Table

Every December, my mother added leaves to the table,
as her mother did, places for guests with nowhere else
to eat ham or yams, turkey or pies
leaking juices through latticed crusts.
They circled our table, hair parted,
forks angled, laps napkined in.

When the last dollop of whipped cream melted
on tongues, my mother passed out baskets,
unlabeled packages. Dad roasted
chestnuts gathered from our yard.

Anyone might have thought we were family,
bundled in parkas at the door,
waiting for cabs or warming cars.
I remember wind tangling their hair,
arms clutched around scarves and leftovers,
their shoes worn. Their names gone.

Hands

Of a thousand hands
I'd know my father's,
long fingers shaped like oars,
the index scar,
the flat, grooved nails,
hands that fixed the doll's arm,
mended Whisker's ear, checked homework.
Those hands grated romano over Sunday pasta,
curled around glasses of wine
he toasted with at dinner,
or opened to offer the sweetest mulberries,
the ripest figs from his trees.

Once he kept a parsley caterpillar
so I could watch it emerge from its cocoon.
The jar was too small, though;
the wings dried with a crease.
It walked the long ramp of my father's hand,
off balance at takeoff.
It fanned and fanned,
but the crease would not unfold,
the wings could not lift.
My father set it in the grass,
and we watched it walk
the short runway of its life,
a tiny lopsided glider without wind.
My father's hands, like long anchors,
dangled at his sides.

Backyard Wishing Well

The wishing well my father built,
painted to match our house,
with a bucket on a rope,
heard wishes and secrets
of friends, relatives, and neighbors
who came and returned
with more friends. Sometimes
we saw them from the window
tossing over their shoulders
or in an underhanded flickering arc.
They tossed for trips and boats,
new houses and cars, for Martha's recovery,
Ben's safety, for boyfriends, girlfriends,
prom dates, periods, rings. They wanted
beauty, first place, a better job. They wanted
to win the lottery, to win the war. Some
closed their eyes, kissed their coins,
and didn't tell their wishes. They tossed
for novelty, for chance, for romantic charm.
When the well went dry, my father went down
to make repairs, dig deeper, but water
didn't return. Only a trickle kept the ground wet.
After that, he rescued fouled balls, a lost ring,
and our cat, meowing from a squat at the bottom,
but we kept on wishing and tossing while the coins
arched and stacked and sank into the mud.

Deer Hunting

As soon as we waved away
the last of my father's exhaust,
tent and bedroll crowding the back window,
Mother called Chicken Delight for delivery,
ready to settle in for the annual weekend
when we did anything we liked.
She was afraid to stay alone, she claimed,
but I always insisted she go first
down the hallway from kitchen to bedrooms
where she switched on lights.
Saturday we lingered in dressing rooms,
traded secrets over lunch.
Dinner was artichoke hearts and black olives
bobbing their silky heads while
we crammed swiss and salami
between the darkest rye
and crunched fat-fingered dills
still wet from briny crocks.
By eight we watched vampires or werewolves,
sometimes the late show if it starred George Raft.
When we slipped under flowered sheets,
I thought of Dad, alone with the stars,
the only time quiet was all his,
the only weekend Mother was all mine.

Bringing Home the Wild

One Sunday, Uncle Nene plopped
a newspapered bundle on the table
for my mother: a bloody beaver.
It was one of his regular surprises.
What am I to do with this? she asked
and crossed her arms. *Cook it,* he said.
Good meat in there. I cut off the tough tail.
My mother rolled her eyes, sighed,
said, *Uno struzzo,* and dropped it in the sink.
A few slits and she skinned it, as though
taking off a tight sweater, and slid it into saltwater.
My father and Uncle Nene ambled outside
to examine fig trees and pick tomatoes.
Salt-water soaks always began her game dishes.
From my father, it was hunting game: squirrel
she fried, rabbit she added to red sauce, pheasant
and duck she roasted, deer she sausaged.
Uncle Nene assumed she could cook anything,
including what Aunt Marianne walked away from.
What he brought was anybody's guess:
woodchuck, gopher, raccoon, muskrat.
Mother swore saltwater helped take the wild out,
a taste we frowned at like fishy fish.
The next step she kept secret—a mix of herbs.
A bit of this and that was all she ever said.
None of it ever tasted like chicken except
the rattlesnake. Mostly Uncle Nene gobbled it up

while the rest of us loaded up on the other
meat dish my mother also made just in case.
Mother was the queen of organ meats: beef tongue tacos,
kidney and potatoes, liver and onions, brains with scrambled
eggs, but she drew the line at opossum and skunk and told
Uncle Nene not to consider pigeons, rats, or voles either.
The beaver was greasy and stringy, globules of fat
oozed between the meat, its taste a skanky blend.
Mother said, *Some meats are better left to the predators.*
We drank too much wine, ate more bread, concluded
beaver was a thumbs down. *That's okay,* Uncle Nene
said. *I'll take it home. Have my eye on a badger for next time.*

Sweatshirt Dress

It hung on a Harzfeld's rack with three others,
one in my size. A white sweatshirt dress,

softer than chamois, with bold signatures
of musicians I loved, rock and roll hieroglyphics

covering the front and back: John Lennon,
Eric Clapton, Jimi Hendrix. I wanted it.

I lifted it from its hanger and hugged it.
Too much for a silly sweatshirt, my mother said.

Let's look at these Jonathan Logans over here.
Had she forgotten what the right dress

could mean? I went back to stare
at Mick Jagger's signature and hold

the dress around me again and again —
until they were sold. Tony Lombardo might

have noticed me in this dress at the party —
where the wild ones slipped around to the side

of the house to puff cigarettes and swig
from pints. The boys straddled motorcycles,

leaned against tricked out cars, and wore
the exact right jackets. A warm halo

from the streetlight surrounded their billows
of smoke. I wasn't supposed to be out there

where everyone looked like someone from *Grease*.
Gina Ferrara threatened to call my mom,

tell everyone on Monday. As I turned to leave,
Nancy Ness, chemistry genius certain to be a scientist,

valedictorian, and Miss America, leaned against
Toni Lombardo, wearing my sweatshirt dress.

Crush on the Americano

He folded origami frogs
and turtles in history class,
and we passed them across desks
to girls named on a fold.

One row over, four back,
I watched him stare
at long creamy necks
or tight, angora sweaters.

After class, he shoved
a rabbit or crane into a purse.
Invites to Homecoming. Parties.
Movies. Dinner at the Bristol.

Please wear your blue sweater
tomorrow. Meet me at your locker.
The blessed always bragged
about their notes or lobster dinners.

One Friday, a folded fish
dropped on my desk — my name,
unexpected as flashcards in church.
Winter dance. I had two weeks.

I bought a pink gown. Tall heels.
Tuesday, he was sorry, his words
like thistles. His parents wouldn't let him
date an Italian. *What would people say?*

Hangnail words, words like chapped thumbs
dragged across a bare breast.
Your own kind, my mother said.
What did you expect?

Ragazza

A good Italian woman
will cover her dust-free house
with crocheted doilies,
bear dark-eyed sons,
know what to do
with artichokes and chickpeas.
Her floors will shine.
She will serve tender *braciole*
in her perfect sauce,
make her own cannoli shells,
bake *biscotti* for every wedding.
Supper will be hot at six o'clock.
She will always wear dresses.
She will not balance the checkbook.
He can doze behind the paper
while she washes dishes.
Because she will never leave him,
he will forgive her bulging thighs.
Because he will never leave her,
she won't notice unfamiliar stains.

Italian men always know *ragazze*
who work the fields in Bivona.
For airfare one will come.
In time she will learn English.
In time they may learn to love.

Control

I.

Mother set four sandwich triangles
on our plates, six Pringle chips, six
orange slices, six apple slices
and a cookie. She sat beside me.
The wrens are trying to fly, she said.
They chirp when I talk to them. We
nibbled and watched birds. *Your father
doesn't think Ray's a good match for you.
You wouldn't want to disappoint him.*
I was nineteen. She scooted closer,
hands bunched around an invisible bouquet,
coiffed hair sprayed into place.
We looked out the window in silence. Wrens
chattered. We ate the last orange slice. Peels
curled on plates in smiles, under the slice
of sunlight slanting in.

II.

Twenty years later, my father and I
sit at the same table for Sunday pasta.
We are single again, discussing
what we might like in a mate.
Whatever happened to Ray? he asks.
Did he get married? I look up.
I thought you didn't like Ray?
He blinks. *Who told you that?*

Under the Table

Home on leave, my boyfriend says at dinner,
I can drink anyone under the table now.
Dad and I nod and eat our linguini. He had warned me
war changes a man before my boyfriend left.
My mother drains her lemonade and announces,
I'll take you on. I roar and choke on a meatball.
She has to be kidding. Dad rolls his eyes
and gulps what's left of his wine. Mother drinks
one highball on Christmas and New Year's.

They choose Saturday night. Mother decides
to set up the picnic table in the garage
with a vinyl tablecloth. Easy to splash
a bucket of soapy water on the floor afterward.
He chooses scotch. I'm sure Mother's never tasted
scotch. Dad's in for two—likes a good scotch now
and then. No one hurries. My boyfriend
tells war stories, Mother talks about meeting
Jack Carson and dancing at Drexel Hall. They sip.

By ten, Mother's eyes glassy, they slug away
like arm wrestlers, holding on until they
slam glasses and add another tick mark
on their scorecards. They want the facts right
when they talk about this. They take turns
pouring drinks. I find Dad asleep on the couch
downstairs. I snooze on the other couch
and wonder why Mother isn't sick. Did she
eat a steak and drink olive oil to get this far?

By midnight, I stumble back into the garage
and find my boyfriend throwing up in the bucket.
He says *Margaret, I'm not through yet,* weaves
his way back, sets his head down, and passes out.
Mother finishes the last of her drink and swipes
the table, as if tidying up a bit.

Preparations for an Italian Wedding

You need a long guest list,
seven or eight hundred relatives,
old school friends, co-workers,
the neighborhood grocer,
the gall bladder patient
your mother shared a hospital room with,
the vet who saved your cat.
When she helps with invitations,
your mother will remember more names.
You will lose all arguments.
She will insist on a long train,
high-neck bridal gown.
Forget the simple garden reception.
Your mother will rent the Hilton,
a five-piece band, four tireless bartenders,
and caterers who were once track stars
to serve a four-course dinner.
You will need a white-slotted box
to stuff money envelopes in,
at least thirty cousins and aunts
to bake cookies for guests to stuff
in plastic bags they tote home
after eating their fill, a hope chest
packed with your hand-stitched linens
and, depending on inflation,
about the cost of a house to pay for it.

The night before
you will hope it doesn't rain,
you will wish you had the money
to buy a house or new furniture,
you will think about suggesting
your own daughter elope.

IV

. . . over and over on the sharp blades.

Victims Lose Direction

In a blizzard, snow surrenders its direction,
unsure if it's snow or sleet, one with the wind.
A man once walked through a blizzard to bring me
a yellow rose and a package wrapped just like
a Bicycle deck queen of hearts.
He was unlike my father, except he knew
how to mend the broken, build what he needed.
Once he built a tetrahedron kite we flew
in an open field of wild flowers. With him
I cracked my first lobster, unsure about forks.
He rescued me from the undertow of a barge
when our canoe tipped on the Missouri River.
He helped me raise six baby rabbits
he recovered from a deserted nest.
He sent dozens of yellow roses.
Through that blizzard, his eyelashes iced,
his jeans crusted, he never lost his way.
That took knee-deep rice paddy mud,
unspearing men from pungi pits,
stepping on a Claymore mine.
After months in Army hospitals,
he folded an origami diamond, identical
to the engagement ring inside. But he couldn't
mend nerve damage, soften welds of scar tissue.
In a blizzard, victims lose direction, see
what isn't there, collide with what is,
become one with the sleet pocking away at them.

The bridesmaids wore daisies in their hair,
the groomsmen dress blues. Guests threw
rose petals as we stepped through a saber arch
supported by wounded vets, our smiles
mirrored over and over on the sharp blades.

Red Silk

I
You sent five yards of red silk
woven with white-patterned leaves.
It stretched down the hallway,
a long shimmering train.
I rolled across its soft sheen,
wrapped it in a sari, a sarong,
flapped it until it billowed, then sank
over me, a flutter of moth wings,
and slid down my arms like mercury.
I dreamed it into a kimono, a robe,
before pinning down papery skins
of patterns. A wedding night negligee
would hug curves and pool into yours.

II
As scissors clipped where light glowed
against shadows, a booby trap
exploded. Its hot, broken stars
split you open, rib cage to groin.
Blood arched and runneled
into the jungle's red clay.
The chopper dusted silt into your glistening
wounds. To the hovering soldiers,
you signaled a Churchill V.
The silk pieces slid from my fingers
when the telegram arrived.

III
From hospital windows you watched
acorns fall twice. Surgeons couldn't rewire
the short-circuited nerves in your arm,
mend the double hernia. One testicle,
half a stomach would suffice. The leg
would swell always. On weekends
I couldn't make the flight, I laid
the silk remnant on the pillow,
waiting for your call.

IV
In the third June, I pressed finished
seams, the iron gliding itself, its radiant
glow startling beside the ivory veil.
Your wounds had scarred into stiff
and knobby steel welds. When the negligee
slid across your arm, you felt it
in your fingertips. Scars rubbed against me
hard as a grate.

V
In sudsy water, the negligee
bled in red streams, dye
breaking ties with the silk.
From a hanger, the gown
dripped red puddles on the floor,
drying a pink shadow of itself.

Wedding Night

The downtown skyline swallowed the stars.
On our Hilton balcony, we sipped champagne.
You stared beyond the darkness, strings
of car lights guiding you there. We crawled
between crisp sheets, soon slippery with sweat.
You stared at the ceiling, chewing your nails.
I was a kink in this knot of wounded soldiers,
a phantom limb. Four would go back
to Fitzsimmons for skin grafts, a new arm,
throat surgery, a rebuilt jaw. The rest
would have to return home. I dressed
for the drive back to the recovery ward
in fatigues, huddled around a poker pot,
chugging beer, shuffling green bills,
our apartment filling with stories
I could now recite: Paul's 27 bayonet
wounds, saved by his killer dog;
Whisper ripping out his trachea; Campo
speared in a pungi pit; Company B torching
villages, the children, running flames;
grenades, mortars, Claymores, dustoffs.
Dress blues hung in plastic bags from knobs,
artificial limbs, a heap above empty fifths
rolling into sleeping bags. From Jim Perry's leg,
we drank beer passed around like a long draft.

You scooted up to the table, lifting
that fresh scotch in a toast to them.
I crept into the darkness of our bed,
new sheets singed with cigarette burns,
holding the smell of somebody else.

First Month

A white haze settled on counters in the tiny
apartment kitchen when I sifted flour for
muffins, rolled flaky pie dough. I pureed
in the new blender, stirred sauces with herbs,
diced, chopped, deboned with new Cutco knives.
Meals steamed at the table in wedding china.
Hot biscuits puddled coins of butter by your
empty plate, gravies congealed. Three a.m.
caterwaulings hustled me from sleep.
You serenaded the neighbors with Boy Scout
songs while strumming a golf club guitar, shouted
Army marching drills or slurred how everyone
should come out to see the moon. Ms. Campbell
shook her fist from the window, left taped notes
on our door. I tried to lure you in with leftovers:
stroganoff, t-bones, chicken divan.
Your hair was a smoky bar room
when you lodged your chin in my shoulder,
backed me into the bedroom, unzipped
your fly. No time for the flirt of eyes,
the clasp and nestle of limbs, the sizzle of foggy
kisses once savored on the old airport road
as jets reversed their engines above us.
The moon was a cool white bowl, waiting for me
to whip meringue for a pie. When I reached for it
in the oven, it would be hot and ready
because I'd given it time.

Faces

> *Like a man drunk on the rage*
> *of being alive* - Yusef Komanyaaka

In the photograph we toast a birthday,
two dozen faces clinking glasses, before
liquor loosened tongues, before you punched
the goose egg on Jeff's eye. Jeff or Joe,
I can't attach names to these grins.
Memory is a red welt. In time, it fades
like this party. I remember punches,
the tangle of fallen legs, soggy carpet.
It took four to drag you into the bathroom.
You pummeled the door until wood split,
yanked towel bars from the wall.
The glass votive you smashed
against the mirror streamed hot wax
on the finger towels, across the tiled floor,
in the spider web of cracks mirroring
the phantasmagoria of faces, your masterpiece
of performance art before the truck driver
rendered you unconscious. I remember
the hard draw of breath, pounding feet
rushing outside, the steady line of Fellini faces
staring from car windows as they floated past
until the street was quiet, except the choking
of my own engine as I loped off into the dark.

I bolted and chained the door, but it
was only a gesture. Like splinters
of streetlight, leaking between curtains,
you would find your way in.
By morning, swollen and split-lipped,
you would deliver familiar promises,
broken by dusk with thirst.

Ambush

You returned after three days,
your jacket a sketch of stains,
your face gashed again.
Silhouetted in the doorway,
you rummaged through my purse,
elbowed me away when I lunged
for the strap, and shot out the door.
I trailed in your wake. My lipstick
rolled like a wasted shell. The compact
gleamed a signal in the streetlight.
You sifted through pens, glasses, keys.
What you want is in Chu Lai, I shrieked.
Billfold pictures arched and fluttered
like clipped wings. I scooped them up,
teeth chattering, *You should have had
a second tour.* We stared at each other,
hope unspooling like the thread that wove
the red silk you sent from Danang.
We were braided green,
now dried in a wreath we couldn't untwist,
couldn't make straight again.
We shuddered in darkness.

Separation

In the quiet of separation, the rooms were mine.
No socks huddled around the chair,
no coffeetable rings, no empty cans.
In this tidy quiet, I roamed, touching what
remained whole, dusting where light filled
empty spaces, not expecting you to check in
singing *For What It's Worth*.
You plucked darts from the board to try
for the bull's eye, asked to borrow my car.
The flatbed had dropped its muffler,
your latest car already in salvage.
Your eye on the target for the last dart,
you swore you wouldn't be drinking.
You suggested a round of Liar's poker,
folding a bill between your fingers.
All evening I stood guard, waiting for the tripflare.
I had lit three candles on the same match.
I was watching the cat lick its paw
when the hospital called. Thanatos
had sent you back again. Three times
the only survivor, thrown through the window
before the fist of fire exploded the car,
chose the trapped woman instead,
the other driver wheezing his last breath.
I scraped the windows of a borrowed car.
Dodging scar tissue, surgeons tied off
black sinew across your face, down your leg.

Sitting up, you delivered your favorite line,
I feel like ten million dollars.
If every stitch holding you together were a mile,
I could have snorkeled in Key West
or watched Alaskan salmon return like you.
Instead, I shuttled you back with crutches,
your face a map I'd never travel,
to that quiet space neither of us wanted you to go.

Ghost in Starlight

The heart has reasons of its own. . . . Pascal

Ice clinking like chest medals, you paced
the dark, caught in a space too dense
to pass through, a ghost in starlight.
Your cigarette's coal was a bobbing signal,
indecipherable. I watched from the bedroom,
picking the lock of my own story.
Weeks of street fairs, bead shops, coastal
drives had brought us here to encircled
ground. No party at Peter's would unravel
seams of silence. All those words,
becoming moonstones inside our stomachs,
couldn't ascend to tongues. In that summer
we tried again, your new turf
a thousand miles from home,
we scavenged empty beaches, where waves
had pounded rock smooth. On water
sunlight winked signals we couldn't read.
We surveyed tide pools, our footing
wobbly on mossy rocks. We were left
with what wouldn't wash off, shells
going off in our heads. In that darkness,
you couldn't hurdle bamboo thickets,
tigers feeding on flesh.
A knock at the door granted you retreat
from the swamp we almost crossed.

Streetlight ringing her Medusa hair,
she whispered, how much longer?
Fire in the hole, I wound the sheet tighter.
You slipped into starlight,
the door's lock clicking behind you.

V

Paul Kidwell rode through our yard
yesterday like the Lone Ranger.
He probably ruined your father's grass.
I never knew he had a horse.

All the Time Running

Even when you see it coming,
leave tread prints behind,
you'll wonder about this moment,
this curve at dusk, the dog chasing
a coyote across a field, the coyote
losing ground each time he checks
his pursuer, all the time running
toward the road, toward the woods
on the other side, all of us thinking
we have enough time. Then brakes
yield that rubbery smell of trying.
In that instant the coyote sees you,
his eyes hold all he knows.
When you stand on the shoulder,
you'll see the pool form, the eyes
glaze over, the body heat
shimmer into air; how fast
light subtracts itself.

Rain Elegy

All night the dog whined through strikes
and flashes while rain pelted the skylight
and sang through our gutters.

Morning hung over with lost limbs,
petals stuck to the patio, I steered
the dog across soggy yard, past runoff.

I remembered the summer the flood
sucked your car into the lake. One hand
dangled from the window when they

hauled you out. The dog stared at standing
water and strained on her leash to go back.
A beheaded tuberose spread far its thick scent.

After Signing Releases

The cobalt machine may scare you.
While you wait for the nurse
to speak from another room,
after she lowers your head
like a loaf in a basket,
there are no posters,
no paintings to distract you.
If you close your eyes,
you could be home
vacuuming the rug.
If you can't swallow puree,
tubes keep you from losing weight.
Ice chips cool dry mouth.
When your hair grows back,
the burns may fade,
the inked tattoos might wear off.
Your voice may gargle
like singing into a fan
or puff like air through a straw.
When pain marauds your brain,
the Demerol refills.
You can double the dose.
The photograph before treatment
is a record of how you looked.
You will not be radioactive.
Nothing bad is going to happen.

Chemotherapy

Up from bed after three days,
you reach for a curl to twist —
it drops in your hand.
Your other tightens on my arm.
I lean beside you,
rest my cheek next to yours.
We are quiet like the snow outside.
We watch cardinals spill seed from the feeder.
I mention they've lived here a long time;
you tell me you miss the wrens.
I think of when I straddled the chair
to brush the hair I loved to touch,
the hair where I buried my head
to find the familiar curve in your neck.

Today your hair drops
after twenty strokes
into the sack
waiting under the brush.
I rub the smooth pink egg
your head has become,
hold you tight
as you always held me.
Outside it is cold.

We spend the afternoon
combing and recombing a wig,
trying to find the place inside us
where we know this doesn't matter,
waiting to talk until we do.

Twelve Days on Methadone

*She may hallucinate but will feel
no pain from the cancer.* Dr. Davidnor

1

A devil flowed from the switch plate
and imitated me pulling my pain.
Then he stuck a gun to his head.

2

Doctors took tests
while I watched from the ceiling.
They kept filling a basket.
Now what was in the basket?
Not a tisket, a tasket.
It was me.

3

I had a big lunch today,
June peas, the best trout,
and five nectarines.
Your father says I only ate grapes,
but he's wrong.
I ate two nectarines
and gave him two.

4

The doctor said my blood is bad,
but I told him we grew up listening
to that. Doctors should be impartial.
Don't step on that kitten.

5

Have you seen all the little people
in this house? They carved initials
in lampshades. I've been watching
them. They live in the couch pillows.
Sit still; one wearing sunglasses
wants on your lap.

6

Paul Kidwell rode through our yard
yesterday like the Lone Ranger.
He probably ruined your father's grass.
I never knew he had a horse.

7

I told your father I wouldn't go
back to the bedroom until the naked couple
came out from under the bed.
It's amazing what happens
when you're gone for a few days.

8

I can't believe you haven't said hello
to your Aunt Mary sitting beside you.
She brought me ice cream.
I told her you and your father
were trying to starve me to death.

9

Last night there was a wall
like in China around the bed.
I knocked on your father's head
until someone answered.
Then he tore it down.

10

Forty people had a party here last night.
They have some illegal ring going.
They offered me ten thousand to keep quiet.
I had to call a lawyer.
Did you know Aunt Lena has a law degree?
Your father tried to stop me
from calling the police, but I got
them here, and they wrote it all down.

11

I couldn't sleep all night.
Those elves across the street
are making puppets for Christmas
on the Kidwell's roof. It's a good thing
kids don't know how foul they talk.

12

I can't understand why your father
lets these animals roam the house.
I couldn't get to the bedroom
until your father moved the cow.
You're looking at me like that again.
Don't start in telling me what's really
happening. I know what I see.

Giant Clown

When I called Mother
to my bed late at night,
she insisted,
There's no clown at your window.
His painted frown,
his tapping, gloved hands,
his polka dot tie
haunted my nights
where I tried, under a flood of sweat,
eyes squeezed tight, to lie still
until he went away.

At six, my nephew,
sheet tugged to his eyes,
called me to his bed.
A giant clown at my window.
There's no clown, I started,
then bit those words.
He's got a rifle and a polka dot tie.
Where?
Right there, he pointed.
Wanna sleep in my room?

When Mother killed cancer pain
with methadone, she was certain
elves built puppets at night across the street,
cows stomped through the house.
Those things aren't really there,
I insisted. *It's just the medicine.*
One afternoon she added,
*Last night I saw a giant clown
outside the window.*
A clown? I asked.
What did he look like?

Margaret's Song

Once she no longer packed school lunches
or concessioned P.T.A. hot dogs,
she bought the piano
she'd promised herself.
Right off she spilled out *Star Dust,*
her chords thick as custard.
On spring days those chords
crowded the house,
tumbled out windows
through the billowing curtains
of Irma Kidwell's kitchen,
found John Enyeart mulching tomato plants,
reached Jack Lyons turning steaks on the grill.
Her hunchbacked fingers pounded songs
she swore no one could write anymore.
Her popular tunes never sounded
quite like melodies anyone hummed,
and she wouldn't play a piece with too many sharps.
She served *Star Dust* daily like dinner salad,
the last song she played.
In winter, her family
gathered around her like a halo,
her chords drowning their *sleep in heavenly peace.*
When she refused all food
and visitors could come only as close as her music,
she still gave herself to the chords,
to a place even pain couldn't reach.

The Importance of Kneading

She said she'd watched
the seasons change from her recliner,
and this one was her last.
She sat like someone
waiting sleepless in an airport.
I pulled out the breadboard,
passed through four mothers,
while she watched icicles
clink on the porch.
It's my turn now, I told her,
to learn the secret of bread.
I wanted to learn from her hands
as she did from her mother.
Don't tell me not today.
She stared at me for a long time.
It's all in the kneading, she answered.
That's all you have to know.

I sifted, warmed yeast with water,
waited in silence with her
while the dough breathed
and seeped over the bowl.
Punch it down, she said,
never having checked a clock.

I buried my hands into the warm mound,
pushed down with the heel of my palm,
over and down, over and down,
until I found the rhythm,
the dough springing back
supple as young skin.

You'll know by the feel, she called to me.
Then you'll never forget;
you'll always make good bread.

She scooted on slippers into the kitchen
when I told her I thought it was time,
still not sure what I had to feel.
Her hands sunk in next to mine.
We pushed together
like the times we played duets on the piano.

There, she said at last,
and I saw in her eyes
what my father said was always alive.

The Occasional Family

They take a long time climbing stairs,
the black-coated ladies,
their puffy dark hair stiff with hairspray,
their squat, square heels
scooting down aisles.
Their closets full of black dresses,
they are always there
to touch cheeks, to pat hands.
Even if they forget names,
they can link families:
Sam's daughter, Rosie's niece.
They toddle through receiving lines,
scholars at grieving, arms open for the hug;
uncle, third cousin, or friend
is always with God at last.
They take close seats to sit it out,
bend fingers in like small cabbages in their laps.
They complain about knees,
touch shoulders in pain,
say they made *pignolate* or bread all day.
They remember how handsome he used to be,
how hard she always worked.
They sit, cloyed with roses, carnations,
lining the walls on thin wire stands,
dripping over the someone finally at peace
while the men hover in the lobby
like awkward birds.

It's familiar like the carpet
worn more in the center,
the ceiling fans quietly turning,
this accidental, occasional family.

Procession

Under the lattice of trees,
shapes of light wink and reappear —
a dance of visible atoms. We wind
through gates to open ground,

remember the tissue wrinkled
in our hand, a mud fleck on a shoe,
wind pushing through a scarf,
the circling of finger on thumbnail.

Silent pause, slam of car doors,
pallbearers stiffen shoulders to lift.
Afternoon is already kneeling
when we move to the front of the line,

dancing light ready to give night
its thirsty chance. Last words invade
the bubble that has carried us here.
Leaf mold surrounds our drowsiness.

VI

. . . already our voices bounce through this empty
house, the walls holding up shadows of late afternoon.

Sorting Things Out

Drawers pulled, a trash bag beside us, my brother
hands me medicine bottles, canceled checks,
instructions for an abandoned clock. We've
worked our way to his old bedroom, once off limits
where he hoarded condoms I found,
pirate books he traded for silence.
The mystery of where he went
lingered in shirts he hung on doorknobs.
After he moved out, I knew my brother
through family dinners and card games,
conversations suitable for a table of faces.
Now we sort through father's estate
as we have most Saturdays, the two of us
unraveling new mysteries: old coins,
unlabeled seeds, birthday cards from widows,
a clove and a toothpick in every jacket pocket.
Today we are sock-footed, recalling crowds
he drew when he tangoed at weddings,
the time I wouldn't move off the driveway,
so he peddled over the teacup in my hand.
After discovering the Mic-O-Say bag,
he sings me camp songs, tells me
the meaning of his and Dad's Indian names.
We try on Dad's hats, tip them back
with old hangers, side step, shoulder to shoulder,
before we lug trash bags to the next room.

My Father's Nightstand

I empty the dead drawers
and sort what my father kept close:
Chapstick, shoestring, book of stamps.
Flashlight, two keys, Allen wrench.
Electrical tape, dental floss, six wire nuts.
Union patch, click pens, notepad.
Six cloves in a baggie, two rolls of Lifesavers.
Four pencils, sharpened with a penknife.
Needle stuck in a spool of black thread.
Fifty-year reunion program tucked in a *TV Guide*.
Mic-O-Say bag, *Star* clippings, six obits.
Two labels: *From the Wine Cellar
of Sam Cusumano. No Sugar Added.*
American flag, 4-leaf clover, rabbit's foot.
Recipe for Anisette, recipe for tanning hides.
Ben Gay, cough drops, a Colt 45.
Beside the phone, cap missing,
an empty bottle of nitroglycerin tablets.

Winemaking

Rows of stacked crates
bled grape juice
on the basement floor
until the right day, when press spikes
broke through wrinkled skins,
mashed out a flow of juice
flooding across wooden slats
into buckets we carried to barrels
until our soles were suction cups
on a floor scattered with stems.

Uncle and Father kept
bottles of their best years
stacked on a shelf
above their barrels.
From first pressing
to final cap,
they savored swigs
until they sampled all.

Later I loaded grapes,
carried buckets
when my father inherited the press,
my own barrel beside my brother's.
I went home wrapped in fermented scent,
hair sticky with twigs.

Now my brother packs up
winepress, barrels.
He will take his inheritance home,
try for a good year
with his own sons.
Before packing the shelf,
we swig from a good bottle,
first time without Father
who could save it all
if it started to turn,
clear it if it went cloudy,
Salvatore who knew the right day
to bring wine to the family table.

Estate Sale

She points to ruby glass, Dresden bowl.
She's called collectors, tagged lampshades,
every dish we're leaving behind. The attic
has reassembled in the hearth room.
Rows of tables pour out a past.

Outside a crowd waits for wingbacks,
tea sets, *Pinkie* and *Blue Boy* framed.
By eight they're digging through tool chests,
bargaining for bedspreads, fishing rods.
Someone swigs from a whisky decanter.

Among them, I've volunteered to punch
the adding machine. I need to see who'll
hang our ornaments, snag that wobbly stool.
All day trucks chug up the street, bookcases
and end tables covered with our prints.

By five I've stacked my second thoughts
under the card table with the sacks:
Nonno's nut bowl, his jeweler's loupe,
Mother's tatted doilies, Dad's pocketknife.

Tomorrow we'll settle receipts, find a home
for the last chair. Already our voices bounce
through this emptying house, the walls
holding up shadows of late afternoon.

The House

I.

Father at the window,
fingers gripping the sill,

eyes sharp on the back fence,
asks if I want the house.

It's a good house, he says,
never looking at me.

Sell it, I say, make
life a smaller parcel.

Too much to move, he answers,
as though time were a short straw.

II.

From the kitchen window
I stare at the yard,

alone with the house
he left behind.

Last spring I cut back
the forsythia without asking,

apologized, sure he'd say
I killed it.

He liked the cleared space.
Yellow nubs are ready to open.

III.

The lawyer asks
if I want the house,

says it's best to sell.
I come for mail,

come to check things,
to sit in kitchen sunlight,

to water African violets
I haven't taken home.

Yesterday I packed
a dozen black sacks,

set them by the curb,
one heartload at a time.

Tuberoses

I. Family

Mother sets aside her crocheting,
the afghan a blanket in her lap,
washes cups, leaves the sink clean.
Father finishes his crossword,
rubs his eyes, gives away his yawn.
Before he locks up, he steps outside
to look at stars.
I earmark my chapter,
hear the lock click.
We meet in the hallway to say good night.
The thick scent of tuberoses
slips through our windows.
All night their fragrance
slides within easy dreams.
The attic fan blurs out
the sounds of sleep
one room apart.

II. After the Funeral

My father fidgets in his chair,
alternates his crossword
with turning pages,
stares at crocheted pillows.
He lifts his glasses to yawn.
He talks about fishing, walking.

I sit in my mother's chair,
wear her Pendleton jacket,
alternate needlepoint
with staring at her crochet hooks
stacked in their box.
I promise to stay a few days,
get things in order.

We leave the sink clean,
the stove light on as she did,
set anything we move back in its place.
We hug in the hallway.
When he starts the attic fan,
the scent of her tuberoses
seeps through our windows.
He steps outside to look at stars.

III. One

It's been a summer
packing boxes, clearing out
the clothes of the dead,
thumbing through dust
of attic and basement,
transplanting before
Father's house sells.
Now in August, beneath my window,
the blooms are out there
on their long, thin stalks,
a cluster of trumpets
holding their notes.
A little wind tonight
could nudge them
to blow their scent
across the sill,
perhaps trick my memory
into easy sleep.

Salute

I slit the last bag
of Father's crappie,
let the odor sift up
from the sink,
an imprint
of his last summers,
when he sandwiched walking
and meals together
around fishing.
The freezer date,
markered in his even print,
now fading like a watercolor,
was only a month
before my uncle found him —
his face still pink
when I arrived,
no different than Sundays
when he napped,
his flat fingers
interlaced across his chest.
My uncle covered him with a blanket
while I stood waiting
as though any minute
he might open his eyes.
Only hours before
we had tapped wineglasses,
salute,

shared antipasta and linguini,
hugged goodbye before I drove away.
Now I cover the white fillets
with tarragon, lemon, dill,
enough for two to eat.

In a Season of Absence

We plowed under the familiar
with the blackened basil leaves.
Now abandoned recipes wait
on the counter. Here is the absence
of cinnamon and sage, biscotti
and wine. Shadows settle
into empty chairs around this table
where no candlesticks soften
the room. Plants sent to hold us up
crowd this space. In the peace plant,
a cobra arches its hooded head.
The single gardenia lifts its odor
to everything unanswered. Night
is silent, except the echo of a seed
in its hollow pod. We stare
through the window, trolling
an empty sky, black as the earth
our feet tamped back into place.
Stars do not feed the masses.
The wilderness has found us out.
Darkness widens our pupils.

VII

We mix things up when we tell
how it once was, someone saying,
That's not it, eager to offer another version.

New Starts

Uncle Phil says he doesn't cover them anymore,
shows me his fig trees, grown from starts
my father gave him years ago. *Eight years,*
I tell him, since I've eaten a fig plucked warm
from trees that reached over our heads.
A special gift, my father said
when he packaged figs in baskets.
I couldn't imagine it, then, the figs
weighty and full, abundant at meals.

My Uncle's trees are short like bushes.
They die back when winter comes.
He's potted two cuttings for me,
one the blue, one the white mission fig.
He advises mulch and manure.
*You don't have to cover them
as your father did.*

I recall wrapping mummies
against Missouri snows.
With a hand like my father's,
Uncle Phil plucks for me
one of his seven figs,
a touchstone to summers
of limitless figs, oozing
a honeyed gleam on trays,
always enough for gorging and giving,
enough for the file of ants lured by nectar.

Taste it, my Uncle says.

Small but sweet, it's a private communion
of mixed blessings. Maybe he knows
the weight of this gift as he lifts his eyebrows
and raises his hand in a gesture
I know well. We carry my starts to the car,
the taste of fig on my tongue.

Between Truth and Wish

Superstitions lead a kind of half-life in a twilight world...
we partly suspend our disbelief and act as if magic worked.

-Margaret Mead

My niece drags Mr. Bunny around the yard
in pursuit of our dogs. My neighbor says
her son hung on to a blanket she could
only wash while he was sleeping.
Years later, when he had his own child,
she presented her son with the silky scrap
wrapped in plastic. I tell her about a day
my mother and I cleaned the attic.
We rummaged through Christmas bulbs,
bent cookie tins, stuffed animals I'd collected.
We tossed turtle, fox, panda. *Bed ornaments,*
Mother said, *except the black dog you carried*
everywhere. I lifted the shapeless mound,
its limp head drooping over a fuzzless shoulder.
I took it to put in my cedar chest
with the wool muff I don't remember.
Across the yard my niece is serving tea
and rock cookies to Mr. Bunny and the dogs,
lying beside her on a blanket.
She scolds Mr. Bunny for taking three cookies.

My neighbor and I return to our gardens.
I weed around parsley, scatter a seed head
in the bare spots for the next crop.
Unhooking a clinging caterpillar,
I remember wearing my mother's Pendleton jacket
for two weeks after she died. Dad's cuff links
I slipped inside a medicine bag necklace,
half-lives I needed between truth and wish.
I gather up pruners, basket of basil and bergamot,
ready to take us in for peaches and cinnamon toast.
Reyna and the dogs have fallen asleep,
her head on Zinnia, her feet across Zeke,
Mr. Bunny tucked under an arm.

Beyond a Window of Light

Yesterday the dog lay his muzzle
on the rug, one paw on my leg,
his signal for petting, his eyes flat
as my aunt's when she sunk
in her chair, staring beyond
the window of light
she once reflected.

Today, Zeke bends to one side
as he circles the yard.
He casts no shadow, seeks no shade,
though the sun bears down.
Soon he's ready to descend,
past the rug's ladder of light,
where the basement floor absorbs
his heat. Like my aunt, no position
cushions what grows inside.

All evening, while I prune
spent blossoms, his shrill whine
picks through darkening silence,
rising above the scent of gardenia.
I clip leaves of amaryllis. It is time
to let the bulb rest in the earth.
In winter it will again
be a red heart, radiant
against falling snow.

Scimeca's

I still drive across town for romano,
a fresh chunk I grate at home,
for black and green olives ladled
from crocks, for family-made sausage,
wrapped in butcher paper loaves,
weighed on an old-fashioned scale.
It's a family business, an old grocer and son
caught between frozen pizzas, low-fat dinners
and the old way: fresh ricotta, gallons
of olive oil, bins of rigatoni, penne.
My Uncle Nene, two blocks from the grocer,
weighs moving to a condo against staying
near his sister and the community center
where friends talk about the old days.
When I gather homework from my crowded
classroom, I weigh their faces against
former classes of waving hands.
Although sometimes I am the tipped end
on a scale, like Mr. Scimeca's son,
I am always weighing toward the balance
of how things are. With new lessons,
I still teach my students, my Uncle Nene
stays in the old neighborhood, and I make
my jaunts to Scimeca's so my red sauce
will taste like my Nonna's as my mother's did.

When I Am in My Kitchen

for Jeanne Marie Beaumont

Under my palms, dough rises on Nonna's breadboard.
Knives, dependable as good clocks, ease through
fish and avocado, chop onions or eggs into dice.

I mince and mash, sauté and stew,
sift and fold, wield spatulas and spoons.
With metal whips, I coax froth and foam.

I slip basil into marriages of garlic and olive oil,
know dash from smidgen or pinch.
I grate and grind, zing zest, and flip.

I'm not afraid of cardamom and coriander, fennel
and bay. I tuck dill into hummus, know the ménage of
rosemary, sage and savory; cinnamon, nutmeg and clove.

I remember mother's meringues, the melt
of her teacakes, the meld of her stews —
and Nonna and her pots heavy and true,

her palm measuring salt, its immutable truth,
its briny clip in the mouth, its promise to preserve.

Zia Rosie Lies Down with the Facts

At ninety, Josie lay down,
crossed breadmaker's hands, said,
I'm committing myself to Jesus,
and took her last breath.
That's what Zia Rosie said.
Beata Madre, I was standing right there.
She was the last zia to remember the huckster
backing his truck into Nonna's yard
to sell eggplants and melons, last
to remember the Birmingham farm
where Zia Sadie rolled the still into the creek
when the *ispettori* arrived, the boat trip
to America, Nonna begging raw fish
for four daughters under eight. *She chewed*
the raw fish and fed them like birds
so they wouldn't throw up, wouldn't die
like those throwing up blood, never seeing
Ellis Island. Chew, chew, chew,
she told them and tore off the good parts
of biscuits marbled with mold.

Now, we gather around Zia Rosie's headstone,
say she was the last zia to remember Easter *biscotti*
shaped like doves, Nonna's fresh mozzarella,
neighbors drinking whey as tonic, Bay the cow.
The *cugini* tell stories third hand,
Papa's horse ride to Bivona to propose,

Nonna's train ride with Uncle Carmello,
our memories of zie crossing
generous arms over mantles
of aproned breasts, meals of ravioli,
cannoli dipped in *cioccolato.*
We mix things up when we tell
how it once was, someone saying,
That's not it, eager to offer another version.

The Last Shot

Colt 45. M-16. Glock 19.
My brother and I watch *The History of Guns*.
Diagrams and battle scenes,
explain the ways of war. I learn
the dominance of an Uzi, the clout of a Luger.
My brother points at guns he's owned,
before he oiled and wrapped each one
to send home with his sons, before
his doctors started another treatment.

Last summer I lined up with his children
to shoot a Coke can with his AK-47.
He insisted on where we pointed our toes,
pulled back our shoulders, slumping
under the rifle's heft. Whether we hit
dirt or can, we handed off the gun,
changed by the force of that bullet,
eager to see my brother shift and nod approval.

He wishes he'd taught me a better feel
for a trigger, the upper hand in the site.
He thinks I should own
at least one gun. Snub nose. P-32.
The borrowed BB gun doesn't count.

On that summer day, he stood so small,
his head hairless, the perfect marksman
now a shadow leaning. With a patch
over one eye, he shot his last time,
the kick knocking him off his feet.
The war inside him using up his arsenal,
his t-shirt a white flag billowing,
he grabbed the side of the shed and hung on.

At the End

for Anthony

The tumor dropped
into the surgeon's hands

like a football, but migrants
ate his lungs and logic.

He believed his wife a spy,
his daughter an informant.

He told me to record his
story of the diamond heist

when the government
sent him to investigate.

We took turns standing
around him at the end.

We didn't light candles.
We didn't hold hands.

His eyes circled the ceiling
all afternoon as though

lifeboats or long arms
were helping him along.

Aloud he said, *Paul Newman,
Walt Disney, Monte Hall.*

The quiver in his neck
slowed. Memory

unbuttoned itself
and floated off like a ribbon

slipping out of reach
taking all we had left of him.

VIII

I can't remember what I read anymore, so that's no good.
I started the same book over every day for three weeks.

Aunt Mary Postulates One Sunday at the Nursing Home

You look like your mother today. You cut your hair!
It's nice enough, but you need pouf on top.
We don't have faces for flat dos. See how
Jimmy combed my hair. I've got pouf.
He's such a good son. And I'm wearing
Elizabeth Taylor's cocktail ring.
Jimmy bought it for me on late night TV.
Jewelry of the Stars. I'm getting Ava Gabor's
brooch next. Boy, she had a lot of affairs,
but she had great jewelry. Speaking of affairs,
Marie Coleman was having one, three doors
down from us, and nobody knew. I don't get it.
Chi lo sa? People could have affairs in here at night.
No one ever comes around to check on us. We could
stop breathing and no one would know.
Necrophiles could neck in here all night long.
Never saw any reason for affairs. The jewelry
they get would be nice, but boy, the sex:
just a bunch of fiddling around in the dark.
What's the big deal? I'd rather go dancing, wear
a mink coat, yeah, white ermine, and diamonds.

I Bring Aunt Mary a Christmas Tree

Oh, what a good Italian woman you are.
You've baked *biscotti* and iced them nice,
pink and green just like I love. And they
taste just like your Aunt Rosie's. I wear
that lap quilt you made me to dinner.
I'm afraid someone might take it, though.
I can't believe all of the stuff you bring.
I loved the pizza and the *pizzelle*,
but I don't have anywhere to put
those family pictures. You can take those
home. I don't recognize some of them.
What's that behind your back? A little tree?
You call that a Christmas tree?
It's nice that you put blinky lights on it
and decorated it with reindeer and candy canes,
but it's not more than a foot tall! *Troppo piccolo.*
Uncle Johnny brought home big trees.
Sometimes we had to cut the tops off.
I used to put tinsel and ornaments on the tree.
They were big and beautiful. Ask Jimmy.
This hotel is too small. I'll be glad when we
go home. These *pigra* maids take forever when I ring.
Uffa! What's that? A crystal star? Too many lights.
Shut that thing off before I quit breathing, and don't
hang that mistletoe in the doorway. I don't want
some old coot in a wheelchair grabbing me
on the way to dinner. We've got enough

nearly naked men here. You have no idea
what they're like when you're gone.
That's what you get in a cheap hotel, but Jimmy says
the room's paid for the month. My eyes are closing.
Come back next week. Leave the tree. It's better
than no tree. When's Christmas anyway?

Aunt Mary Wants a Chef

I'm glad you're early. You won't believe this restaurant.
These people need help. We get white linen on Sunday,
and the wallpaper's nice enough, but the food? *Terribile.*
I think they toss meat in boiling water and throw in
canned vegetables. Then pudding or stewed fruit.
Once in a while, bad pie—all crust and no cherries
or apples. I told Jimmy he needs to teach the cooks
a couple of sauces, something with wine or at least
a little oregano. I told them, *My son is a chef. He can
help you. We used to own a restaurant.* They thought
I was *pazza*. That's what they think we all are. Besides,
Jimmy could use some part-time work. He quit his job
to come here every day. He could make us a nice roast,
a pie somebody would eat, or a batch of *cannoli*.
Sono Buoni. Remember how we used to sit
on the porch and put butter on our crackers? *Gustoso*.
These people don't know what a Country Club cracker is.
Saltines. *Per favore!* We used to make good biscotti too.
Sometimes Jimmy makes some and brings them
warm. I'd like some now. Maybe you could take us out
next Sunday to a different restaurant, bring a bigger car
so I can get my wheelchair in, maybe bring a nice girl
for Jimmy. He's never going to find someone here.
Time for lunch. You can come and see for yourself.

Aunt Mary Complains about Entertainment

Thank God you're here. You need to talk
to the stage manager. I can't get Jimmy to do it.
Last week they rolled in a piano. Kids
sang about spiders and rain. *Che palle.*
They call this entertainment. I thought they'd play
show tunes, Sinatra, good songs people like.
You wouldn't believe it. *Incredibile.*
They had a cage of wrens, hopping around
chirping. Made my ears ring! Jimmy said
they were finches, but what's the difference?
I'll bet this stage manager has never been to Vegas.
Someone needs to take him out on the town. Maybe
you and Jimmy can take him to a club, talk to him
about programs for old people. Give him tips,
like they could show us old black and white movies.
They're good. Wear a cute dress and curl your hair
when you take that man out. We'll all be grateful to you.
Take Jimmy. And make him wear a tie.

Aunt Mary Looks for Company

Oh, you caught me, staring out the window.
I don't know why I do it. *Chi lo sa?* I wonder myself.
You brought me a book? I can't remember what I read
anymore, so that's no good. I started the same book over
every day for three weeks. And those TV shows—*terribile*.
I never liked soaps. Nonna watched *Guiding Light* every day.
Not me. I like *Wheel of Fortune* and *The Price is Right*,
but Bob Barker got old. He used to be handsome. Anyway,
that's only two shows. I like a little chat now and then,
but most of the people here don't talk at all. The only place
I can get any conversation is at the beauty shop.
These aides keep trying to get me into those craft rooms.
I could probably talk to someone there, but what a joke that is.
The one time I went I thought we were gonna play poker
or pinochle. They wanted me to glue shells on felt.
I can't believe they expect anyone to do that. *Perfido!*
They make my ass tired. I don't need to talk to someone
that bad. *Che palle!* I can talk a little with Ms. Bell at dinner.
She said her neighbor divorced his wife because she kept
tossing out his cold cuts and serving him tuna noodle
casserole instead. Uncle Johnny always liked what I cooked.
I liked what he cooked too—except for that calamari.
Orrendo! I saw that stuff before he cut it up.
No way. You might as well eat rubber bands. See, already
my eyes are closing. I'll get back with you later.

Aunt Mary Wonders about Guests in the Hall

Today I'd like a piece of coconut cream pie.
Why don't you see what you can do about it.
You'd think that wouldn't be too much to ask
of a decent hotel, but this place reminds me
of Aunt Jean's apartment after Uncle Ray died—
or those old boarding houses full of bedbugs,
rooms so small tenants sat in the parlor
and talked about clerk jobs or duct tape or poodles
they once had. You're too young to remember.
Every Wednesday Jimmy pushes me
through these halls to get my hair fixed.
Old people lined up in wheelchairs
along the walls. They stare straight ahead
like they're watching a movie. I asked Jimmy
what they were watching. He said, *Space.*
What's that mean? Some new show?
They're like mannequins in Macy's windows.
Some never say a word. Mrs. Bell says, *gatatow*,
whatever that means, and *help* over and over all day.
È triste, she can't put words together anymore.
Why do they let guests see that? *Che peccato.*
They don't bring them in the restaurant to eat.
I don't know where they eat. Maybe they don't.
I carry my beaded bag close to me all the same,
while Jimmy pushes me, and cover my legs
with that lacy lap quilt you made me.
I may feel bad, but I still try to look good.

See how nice Jimmy painted my nails?
What do you think of this lipstick? Too dark?
Uncle Johnny would tell me the truth.
I wish he were here right now.
He'd find me some coconut cream pie.
We'd have a nice highball together.

Aunt Mary Pines for Shopping

Cute dress you're wearing.
Could use a little lace, though.
I miss rummaging through racks.
I found cute dresses for you, like that
black and red dress from Dillard's.
Piccola bambola. I checked for that sale
every afternoon. I used to shop every day
like Aunt Sarah and Josephine Pisciotta.
I took you too sometimes. You loved
Harzfeld's' Christmas windows. You thought
the moving dolls were real. We ate
finger sandwiches at Peck's, bought
Charl-Mont Annaclairs. Remember that?
I can't drive us anymore. Can't get in a car.
Nobody here takes us shopping. No one
takes us to see holiday lights. It's a sad place at night.
Some people howl. *È triste.* I just pull the covers up.
What's the use? I try to remember when Uncle Johnny
took me dancing. I wore sequined dresses.
Ah, don't ever get old. Don't end up here.
Next time, bring me some of those Annaclairs.

Aunt Mary Reflects on Her Passing

I've been thinking it's time Uncle Johnny
came for me like your Nonna came for your mother.
I've been here long enough. Jim's a good son.
He comes here every day, but he needs a girl
to share an afternoon cocktail with. He needs
to go to the movies with Frank and Jerry.

I told him he'd better make me look good
in my coffin. Make sure my hair gets dyed
and has pouf like I like it. I hate when people say
how good someone used to look. I want people
to talk about how good I looked even dead.

I already picked that pink dress I love
and the real pearls Uncle Johnny gave me.
Plenty of time to plan here while I stare at the wall.
Your mother wanted gardenias, but I want roses.
Lots of 'em. I don't care if they're in season.
Orchids are pretty, but who can smell them?
I want the whole room to smell like roses. I want
a big spray and a coffin blanket of red roses
like Marie Ballante had on hers. At the grave,
we took one when we walked by. I liked that.
I saved my rose. That's what I want. Something
for people to keep. Besides you and Jimmy,
not many left to think about me after I'm gone.

Enough time and everyone dies off. People
remember Jennie's restaurant, but how many
still remember how she took us back in the kitchen
and let us choose from pots what we wanted to eat?
Or that extra pizza or *vino* she brought to the table?
Better make an impression while you're here.
Once they start tossing that dirt on your grave,
you're just a body under a stone.

Mantiglia

My cousin Jimmy hands me
the black *mantiglia* I bought
Aunt Mary thirty years ago,
a tiny rip in the rose and leaf motif.

From sheets of tissue, the clerk pulled
dozens of scalloped *mantiglie*.
He held up to window light
patterns of florals and fruit

for me to choose and carry home
from Florence. Lacy vines
and lilies for myself; iris
and cherries for my mother.

I tuck Aunt Mary's *mantiglia*
next to my mother's and mine,
the one I wore to both their funerals,
all three again combined.

IX

This picture is before my time,
and I have no one to ask.

In Your Own Way

When you show up, Dad, it's always with
that smile that had widows bring
casseroles and need new wall switches.
I find you in the faces of white-headed husbands
waiting near dressing rooms, their laps full of sacks.
I smell you still in your hairbrush and bathrobe,
if I plant too deep, hear your voice in the garden.
When I chop garlic, it's your hands at the knife.
As I stare over water, I see you reeling line back,
your cooler full of crappie.
The first time you returned in a dream,
we lounged on lawn chairs in your basement,
drank your best wine.
Gesturing with paddle fingers,
rocking oars in an air sea,
you said I needed a man.
Today, as we watch gulls skim waves,
my husband lounges beside me,
the man you picked in your own way:
as he nods at my gestures,
my hands are your hands in the air,
your words on my tongue.

Depth Finder

I can't see my husband from the study,
but I know he's at the window looking out,
thinking as he waters the hibiscus.
He loves the silence of his plants
reaching up, new blooms like offerings.
I know he's watching the wind
dipping and lifting the leaves outside.
He knows about wind and direction,
about feeding his sails so his boat
leans and skims towards the dam.
He says little as he stares across the lake,
as though he's listening to the wind's
breath and his own become one.
He needs only a depth finder so we
don't go aground. This is my job,
to monitor depth. At times, I pull
wench ropes. Tonight I hear the water
soaking the plants, the wind setting off
the chimes. I join my husband where
he stares out the window. Sometimes
when I stand on the bow as he glides us
into the cove, I can almost touch what he feels.

Second Chance

My husband sits in his boat in our driveway,
bent on perfecting his new, used Hunter.

He downsized his bigger O'Day for this 20-footer.
The world looks different from a boat parked in a driveway.

I watch him from the window as he dons
his captain's hat, pulls out his binoculars,

and cups his hand over his eyes to look out.
I wonder if neighbors have noticed he isn't

backing down the driveway each morning at seven.
He replaces bolts, sands wood, and tests a new motor,

its propeller spinning in a trashcan filled with water.
He waves to dog walkers then gives them sailing tips.

Tim from across the street climbs aboard.
I come bearing cold drinks, but Greg's tinkering

in the cabin, checking screws, caulking windows.
At night I wake to see him looking at the boat

from the bedroom window, the curtain cloaked
around him in the dark, the boat reflecting moonlight.

Perhaps he's wondering if an older, second-hand boat
can still command respect

                                          if it has a chance

to meet the waves head on.

The Black-dress Ladies Sit Down
With the Cousins At Our Last Uncle's Wake

Only a few remain of the loyal grievers,
the black-dress ladies,
their white halo hair, faces
scrubbed luminous as moonflowers
next to the night of black scarves.
They kneel at caskets, cross themselves,
and bring back every death we can remember.
They hug and kiss us, stroke our hands.
Sometimes they hand us a prayer in an envelope,
a photo or news article they saved for us,
but we know they are the prayer.
Once they sat up all night for the dead
and into the next day and night.
Today they've come to us for the last time.
They barely know our names, but they
tell stories about our parents, our last Uncle.
We are Jasper's daughter or Gina's son,
and Nene's the last of the ten we knew.
It is a time of remembering and nodding.
We will sit for hours but not all night anymore.
They settle into their seats, dresses so long,
not even an ankle, their black shoes
closed, their hands over prayer books.
Short and thick as gnocchi they shape
between fingers, they shake heads,
raise their eyes to what we don't know,

look to their children, or those from the North End
where they've always lived. They speak
in their old dialect about an Italy
they'd never be able to find now.

Finding a Photo in the Attic

My mother, the focus
at a table of eight,

dark circles under her eyes.
Her horsey, woozy grin

and raised glass command
more booze. The others laugh,

eyes half closed. The bald man
next to my mother — a toothless

Red Skelton smile, cardigan buttoned
in the wrong holes — is not my father.

My father grins; a tail of smoke rises
from his unfiltered cigarette.

He leans close to a blonde, peering
over fanned cards covering her face.

My father's hair is black and wavy.
My mother's jacket hugs her tiny waist.

Ankles touching, she's
angled her open-toed heels.

The mother I knew drank
one highball on holidays.

My father made it
with mostly soda.

This picture is before my time,
and I have no one to ask.

Walking Sticks

My cousin and I, making collages
all afternoon and eating chocolate,
retell our favorite family stories.
She tells about the time a pig
trotted into our Nonna's house,
stomped on the presents,
and knocked down the Christmas tree.
I tell about when Nonno Antonio
tried to kill ghosts with a gun.
We browse through magazine pages,
look for scenes and animals to cut.
She finds a page of insects — silkworm,
luna moth, patterned beetle. I tell her
I saw a walking stick on the patio light
last night. She says she'd love to see one.
It's been so long. I say let's go look,
the patio light on, the night black,
but she shakes her head. A glass of wine
has rendered her listless as a queen bee.
After we tidy up our papers and glue, she
drives home. I take the dog out for one last walk.
Two walking sticks on the lamp are mating.

Don't Read in the Dark

> *The eye altering, alters all.*
> William Blake

You'll go blind, my mother said
and switched on a light
every time I sat down to read.

No one can read in the dark,
I laughed and rolled the eyes
I trusted for sharp images.

Yes, no one could read in that far
corner, where dusk lay creased
and folded as drapes in snow,

but plenty of light slanted
through blinds where I sat
with a book and a window.

Today, the optometrist asks,
Clearer on A or B? A or B?

Neither.

It's not about turning a blind eye,
an invisible eye, an eye on a goal.

Stay out of sunlight. Wear
sunglasses, he warns me.
Street signs will be blurry.
Probably shouldn't drive at night.

Last week a jay stunned itself
flying into a window,
broke off part of its beak.

On my walk, birds scatter like tossed
confetti — lift, bend, spin, swirl.

Black Bird

> *The blackbird whistling*
> *or just after.*   Wallace Stevens

The black bird whistles
from Chau's roof each morning
as my dog and I pass.
Whistles and stares.

He isn't a crow, a starling,
a grackle, a cowbird.
Not a raven, doesn't caw,
but he is involved in what I know.

If anyone joins us, he doesn't sing.
He adjusts his feet, tilts his head,
taps sideways like an old typewriter.

His call is half a whistle
of a boy for a girl passing by.
Every morning, half a whistle,
sometimes two or three.

One morning, as I rounded
the cul-de-sac without my dog,
he completed the other half.
Was he waiting for this moment?

The next morning, after a thunderstorm,
he whistled over and over, his same half
whistle, only faster as he danced
back and forth on the ridge of the roof.

I looked where he was staring.

A nest lay in the grass,
the robin eggs broken.
The unready birth of wet curls
stirred in the wind,

and the black bird called over and over
all morning long, and then he was gone.

Gifts

Near the quiet voice of the pond,
a turtle treads his way,
a dragonfly lands at our feet.

Bamboo stalks wave toward
the sky, their hollow tunes
caught in the wind.

Into air the blind inchworm
throws himself, certain
he will land on another blade.

The stone waits to speak;
the spin of leaves
open a new path.

Morning steam rises,
carries with it
all the weight

of our hearts until
they are lighter than air,
until they float like mist.

Month of Ashes

My dog inhales earth for news,
digs up vole skulls, rolls on scent.
It's March. Month of ashes. Month of thorns.

We've come outside to curbed salt
and bare spots where leaves killed grass.
Where we walk, the earth is soggy, uneven.

Pablo trails fresh deer tracks,
marks fence posts and fallen birch limbs,
checks a stir under leaves, movement in grass.

Near the pond, he bolts uphill,
his tail a rudder for making turns,
a gauge of mood at the rustle under briars.

Windblown sticks stack themselves.
I think of absence, bread from stones,
rise of awakened flies, longer hours of light.

We search for something green.
Two hyacinths poke through brown leaves.
A ladybug crawls through a crevice near a snail.

At home, I pack dead marigolds,
acorns, winter's slough into black bags.
Crocuses are showgirls beside a prickly stalk.

Pablo knows where beetles hatch,
how deep the toads, where spiders hunt —
all of us pushing out, re-shoring at winter's end.

Illusions

The basil sent up a stem of buds,
ready to die in June.
I pinched off the top
to grow more leaves.

This fall, a few oak leaves
have curled and floated down, boats
carrying insect eggs to soil, their
parents now spinning in the wind.

In her last moments, years ago,
my mother sat up to greet
her mother before we heard her last
breath press hard toward sound.

After veal and anisette,
my father slipped away
alone at night, his nitro
bottle empty on the floor.

After his last Sunday dinner,
my brother's eyes circled
the ceiling over and over
before his tapping fingers lay still.

Tonight, when frost threatens,
I tuck basil under a sheet, hope
for another batch of pesto,
a reddening of green tomatoes.

Soon winter will seep into earth,
leave us to contemplate
how some can grow new limbs,
some cannot avoid the flame.

Glossary of Italian Words

alito cattivo – wet wool

andiamo – let's go

Anisette – a licorice liqueur

bambola – baby doll

basta – enough

beata madre – blessed mother

bello – beautiful, wonderful

bianche – white

bisnonna—great grandparents

biscotti – cookies

braciole – a rolled, stuffed meat

brutta -- ugly

buffo – funny

bugie – lies

caldo – hot

cannoli – an Italian stuffed pastry

che palle – what a pain

che peccato –what a pity

chiaccierone – chatterbox, gossip

chi lo sa – Who knows?

cioccolato – chocolate

cugini/cugino – cousins / cousin

danza – dance

demoni – demons

dove sei – where are you?

é triste – it's sad

faccia – face
fortunato – lucky
furiosi – furious
gato – cat
giugiulena – sesame seeds
grande – big
grazia – grace
guarda – look
gustoso – tasty
incredibile – incredible
ispettori – police inspectors
oh mio – oh my
orrendo – horrible
mantiglia – lace scarf or head cover
mistero – mystery
niente – nothing
nonna/nonno – grandmother / grandfather
pane – bread
pazza – crazy
per favore – please
perfido – terrible, awful
piccola bambola – little doll
pignolate – a honey-covered cookie
pigro – lazy
pizzelle – a flat-iron Italian cookie
poveri – the poor
presenti – presents
puttana / puttani – prostitute or whore

ragazza / *ragazze* – young girl / young girls
religiosa – religious
salute – to your health, cheers — used with toasts
segreto – secret
sono buoni – they're good
struttura – texture
subdolo – sneaky
sugo – sauce as in Italian red sauce
terribile – terrible
testa dura – hard headed
troppo piccolo – too small
uno struzzo – someone who can eating anything, like an ostrich, with no problems
va bene – okay then
vino – wine
zie / *zia* / *zio* – aunts /aunt / uncle

What The Zie Told Us

Bivona – a small town in Sicily
Cianciano – a small town in Sicily
S. S. Germania – the ship my grandmother sailed to America on with four aunts

Maryfrances Wagner's books include *Salvatore's Daughter, Light Subtracts Itself, Dioramas, Pouf, Silence of Red Glass,* and *Red Silk,* winner of the Thorpe Menn Book Award. Poems have appeared in *New Letters, Midwest Quarterly, Laurel Review, Natural Bridge, Voices in Italian Americana, Birmingham Poetry Review, Louisville Review, Poetry East, Unsettling America: An Anthology of Contemporary Multicultural Poetry (Penguin Books), Literature Across Cultures (Pearson/Longman),* and *The Dream Book, An Anthology of Writings by Italian American Women* (winner of the American Book Award from the Before Columbus Foundation. Work from that book was chosen for *American Audio Prose* and was translated into Italian for *Trapani Nuovo* in Italy). In addition she has published work in many other journals and anthologies. She co-edits the *I-70 Review,* co-edited the *Whirlybird Anthology of Greater Kansas City Writers, Missouri Poets: An Anthology,* and *New Letters Review of Books.* She has served as Co-president of The Writers Place in Kansas City and is active within the writing community. A dog lover, she and her husband, Greg Field, live with Sylvie Plath and Annie Sexton, two dogs they rescued. Maryfrances has taught academic and creative writing as well as mentored, coordinated, and facilitated at all levels. She has lived in the Greater Kansas City area all of her life.

This project was made possible, in part, by generous support from the Osage Arts Community.

Osage Arts Community provides temporary time, space and support for the creation of new artistic works in a retreat format, serving creative people of all kinds — visual artists, composers, poets, fiction and nonfiction writers. Located on a 152-acre farm in an isolated rural mountainside setting in Central Missouri and bordered by ¾ of a mile of the Gasconade River, OAC provides residencies to those working alone, as well as welcoming collaborative teams, offering living space and workspace in a country environment to emerging and mid-career artists. For more information, visit us at www.osageac.org

Osage Arts Community

www.ingramcontent.com/pod-product-compliance
Lightning Source LLC
Chambersburg PA
CBHW030112100526
44591CB00009B/379